T0329365

CAMBRIDGE LIBRARY COLLECTION

Books of enduring scholarly value

Education

This series focuses on educational theory and practice, particularly in the context of eighteenth- and nineteenth-century Europe and its colonies, and America. During this period, the questions of who should be educated, to what age, to what standard and using what curriculum, were widely debated. The reform of schools and universities, the drive towards improving women's education, and the movement for free (or at least low-cost) schools for the poor were all major concerns both for governments and for society at large. The books selected for reissue in this series discuss key issues of their time, including the 'appropriate' levels of instruction for the children of the working classes, the emergence of adult education movements, and proposals for the higher education of women. They also cover topics that still resonate today, such as the nature of education, the role of universities in the diffusion of knowledge, and the involvement of religious groups in establishing and running schools.

Reciprocal Duties of Parents and Children

Displaying her intellectual and literary abilities from a young age, 'Mrs Taylor of Ongar' (1757–1830) enjoyed writing all her life. She had eleven children, of whom six (four of them writers) survived to adulthood. Her published works began with advice books for her own daughters, produced when increasing deafness made ordinary conversation difficult for her. This book, published in 1818, follows her earlier works for young women with a guide to conduct and 'reciprocal duties' within the family. Stern warnings and cautionary tales are given to show the importance of duty to and respect for parents by children, but the parental duties of care in rearing and especially in education are emphasised. Early discipline, lovingly applied, is seen as the key to successful parenting, and its absence is deemed disastrous. Like Ann Taylor's *Practical Hints to Young Females* (also reissued in this series), the book offers fascinating insights into the middle-class ideal of domestic happiness.

Cambridge University Press has long been a pioneer in the reissuing of out-of-print titles from its own backlist, producing digital reprints of books that are still sought after by scholars and students but could not be reprinted economically using traditional technology. The Cambridge Library Collection extends this activity to a wider range of books which are still of importance to researchers and professionals, either for the source material they contain, or as landmarks in the history of their academic discipline.

Drawing from the world-renowned collections in the Cambridge University Library and other partner libraries, and guided by the advice of experts in each subject area, Cambridge University Press is using state-of-the-art scanning machines in its own Printing House to capture the content of each book selected for inclusion. The files are processed to give a consistently clear, crisp image, and the books finished to the high quality standard for which the Press is recognised around the world. The latest print-on-demand technology ensures that the books will remain available indefinitely, and that orders for single or multiple copies can quickly be supplied.

The Cambridge Library Collection brings back to life books of enduring scholarly value (including out-of-copyright works originally issued by other publishers) across a wide range of disciplines in the humanities and social sciences and in science and technology.

Reciprocal Duties
of Parents and Children

ANN TAYLOR

CAMBRIDGE
UNIVERSITY PRESS

CAMBRIDGE
UNIVERSITY PRESS

University Printing House, Cambridge, CB2 8BS, United Kingdom

Cambridge University Press is part of the University of Cambridge.
It furthers the University's mission by disseminating knowledge in the pursuit of
education, learning and research at the highest international levels of excellence.

www.cambridge.org
Information on this title: www.cambridge.org/9781108076258

© in this compilation Cambridge University Press 2015

This edition first published 1818
This digitally printed version 2015

ISBN 978-1-108-07625-8 Paperback

RECIPROCAL DUTIES.

Published June 1, 1818, by Taylor & Hessey, 93 Fleet Street.

RECIPROCAL DUTIES

OF

PARENTS AND CHILDREN.

BY MRS. TAYLOR,

AUTHOR OF MATERNAL SOLICITUDE, PRACTICAL HINTS,

&c. &c. &c.

"Children, obey your parents in all things; for this is
well pleasing to the Lord.
"Fathers, provoke not your children to anger, lest they
be discouraged."   *Col. iii,* 20, 21.

LONDON:

PRINTED FOR TAYLOR AND HESSEY,

93, FLEET STREET.

1818.

T. MILLER, Printer,
5, Noble-Street, Cheapside.

CONTENTS.

Contents

RECIPROCAL DUTIES

OF

PARENTS AND CHILDREN.

INTRODUCTORY CHAPTER.

BEHOLD that lovely cherub in the arms of its fond mother! It has been but a few months in existence, yet it has already learned to recognise its best friend: her faithful bosom is the receptacle of all its tiny sorrows and joys; its hopes are derived from her experienced kindness; its fears are allayed by her protecting care: on this well known being it depends, for all that can soothe and delight. The utmost ingenuity of the nurse, though aided by the delicious morsel, or the glittering toy, is

B

of little avail when *she* appears, in whom is concentrated every gratification of which its infant mind is susceptible. Soon, under her assiduous care, its bodily and mental powers begin to expand; its joys and its woes are more intelligibly expressed; it grows fertile in schemes and contrivances for its own amusement (as yet it dreams not of existing for any other purpose); in these the fond parent participates, and is consulted on all occasions without reserve. In the frolicsome gambol she renews her interest, and again enjoys the pleasures of infancy with a double zest.

" She feels and owns an interest in their play,
Adopts each wish their wayward whims unfold,
And tells, at every call, the story ten times told."

The companion in health, the watchful, assiduous, and anxious friend in sickness, the prime of a mother's days imperceptibly glides along, bearing away her personal graces, and not unfrequently leaving her constitution a wreck.

As infancy ripens into childhood, her duties alter, but her zeal continues una-

bated : she perseveres in accommodating her
services to the growing necessities of her
charge, till that important period arrives,
when childhood emerges into youth, and a new
epoch commences in the maternal feelings.
Then, then it is, that the subjects of her
solicitude begin to seek their gratifications
from other sources; and in proportion to
their success, are prone to forget whence
they were once derived : confidence gradually
declines ; and that society which heretofore
comprised all that was desirable, becomes,
perhaps, irksome,—a burden and a restraint :
so that the reserved and distant being we now
contemplate, could scarcely be identified with
the smiling cherub of former days.

The brute creatures, like the human species, attend their young progeny with anxious
solicitude; and when their services are no
longer necessary, the parent first breaks
the tender tie, and chases them away to
know them no more : but human ties can
alone be dissolved by death ; and whatever
alienations ensue, they are not warranted by
nature, or by nature's God. " Honour thy
father and thy mother," is a command coeval

with the existence of our parents; and should
be as deeply engraven on the human heart,
as once it was on the table of stone written
by the finger of God. If, unhappily, these
characters have been erased, the loudest pro-
fessions of religion, or the strictest pretensions to moral rectitude, are as the sounding
brass, and tinkling cymbal: it is vain for
those to profess love to God and their neighbour, who are remiss in affectionate duty to
the individuals whom He has placed in the
intermediate space, and distinguished by the
peculiar honour of assuming His character,
who styles Himself the universal parent.

Filial attachment is not a virtue of difficult attainment; indeed, it is not a quality
to be acquired, but is inherent in our nature.
It is not to be *planted*, but *cherished;* and is
distinguished beyond all other virtues by promises of temporal blessings: nevertheless,
there are parents who have to take up the
lamentation, and say, " I have nourished
and brought up children, and they have re-
belled against me."

That the causes of such complaints may,
in most instances, be traced to early indul-

gence, or to a want of judicious, enlightened management on the part of the parent, forms no reasonable excuse for the conduct of an undutiful child ; but let parents, who, in the bitterness of their hearts, lament the unkindness or unmanageableness of grown-up children, look back to a time to which their children's memories can scarcely extend ; to the period of their childhood and infancy, when the engaging pettishness was winked at, and the amusing rebellion was half encouraged ; or when, immersed in cares of very inferior importance, or in recreations which every *good* mother will cheerfully resign, the nursery was consigned to hirelings. Let them call up such recollections, (which, we are persuaded, the memories of most complaining parents might furnish) before they feel surprised at the result, or consider their present circumstances as unaccountable.

But, more especially, let those parents who are only commencing their task, who have yet the future peace and happiness of themselves, and of their children, in a great degree at their disposal, recollect, that there are *reciprocal* duties between parents and

children; and that those of the former stand
first, both in order and importance. Let the
fond mother survey the lovely infant in her
arms; let the delighted father contemplate the
rosy groupe around his kness, and reflect with
feelings of deep and anxious responsibility,
that the real welfare of these *darlings* depends, as the means, almost entirely upon
themselves,—upon their affection taking at
once the right direction. That fondness, indeed, which excites parents to injudicious
indulgence, is pure selfishness; that which
impels them to restrain and educate them,
alone deserves the name of parental love.

There is no view which a reflecting mind
can take of this subject, but what is calculated
to impress upon it an idea of its vast importance. There is no relation we may bear to
society, which has not an imperious claim on
those who are furnishing it with new members; no period, however remote, which present tuition may not affect: and shall the
rearing of a family be deemed a light matter?
shall its duties yield to every frivolity that
solicits attention?—Should not this rather be
the language of parental solicitude? "I have

so many human beings—so many immortal
creatures committed to my charge; I know
the snares, temptations, and trials which have
beset my own path; I anticipate similar ones
in theirs : already they manifest their propensity to evil, their averseness to good : amid
all their diversity of tempers and dispositions,
I perceive one characteristic symptom of their
corrupt original. O, thou God of the families of the earth! shall I ever give Thee
reason to repent of having granted me children, as thou once didst of having created
man, because of his evil imaginations? Who
is sufficient for these things? Thou that
givest wisdom to those who ask it, teach me
to train up these children for Thy service
here on earth, and for the enjoyment of Thee
in the world above!"

For those who are thus earnest and sincere, there is abundant encouragement: they
will not labour in vain, or spend their
strength for nought; but will assuredly reap
some fruits of their anxiety and toil, although, perhaps, not of the kind or degree
which they had anticipated. Evil precepts

and examples have *their* reward; and may
not judicious discipline, and pious instruction,
anticipate some reward also ?

Yet, it must be confessed, that the best
instructions, although founded on genuine
piety, sometimes fail, from want of sufficient
skill to direct them. Parents cannot acquit
themselves well in this arduous task, if they
have not acquired the habit of reflecting, and
observing if their minds are unfurnished, and
their knowledge of men and things narrow
and circumscribed. Such persons deem it
sufficient to tell their children, that this is
right, and that is wrong, without being able
to discover the motives which actuate or to
warn of the consequences likely to result. Is
it any wonder, if, while children enjoy the
present gratification of an evil action, they
resolve to repeat it, in spite of admonitions
which do not excite their interest, or attract
their attention? in spite even of chastise-
ments, for which they are not taught to see
the necessity, or discern the full meaning ?

Besides these fundamental duties, there
are others which belong both to parents and

children, during the succeeding stages of life,
and which extend to its latest period. To
explain and enforce some of these subsequent
obligations, is the more particular object of
the following pages.

CHAP. II.

" Cool age advances venerably wise,
Turns on all hands its deep discerning eyes,
Sees what befel, and what may yet befal,
Concludes for both, and best provides for all."   POPE.

" Children's children are the crown of old men, and
the glory of children are their fathers."   PROV. xvii. 6.

YOUNG persons who are naturally disposed to
" rise up before the hoary head," will rarely
be remiss in filial respect and obedience; but
where this amiable sentiment of reverence for
age does not exist, parents themselves are generally the first to feel the absence of it.
Surely something beyond an internal expression of respect is intended by that divine in-
junction, something perhaps more honourable and advantageous to the giver than to

the receiver of such homage; for if that precept, "lean not to thine own understanding,"
be generally addressed to all ages and condi-
tions, how peculiarly does it apply to those
who are destitute of experience, and all its advantages, and who might derive the greatest
benefit from a respectful deference to the
judgment of those who possess them!

Should any young reader be disposed, like
Rehoboam, to give preference to the counsel of
the young brought up with them, rather than
to that of persons of superior years and experience, a similar result may be the consequence; for it is worthy of remark, that Rehoboam was forty years old, and perhaps in his
own estimation arrived at the zenith of mental
capacity as well as of bodily strength: but sacred
history unites with daily experience to evince
the fallacy of such self-sufficiency, and to prove,
that while the faculties remain unimpaired,
there is no period of our existence in which
we may not hope to make advances in wisdom
and knowledge. I am convinced there are none
of my young readers, who do not conceive *themselves* to have derived benefit from experience,

in proportion to their years, whatever the opinion of others may be concerning them; why then should they conclude that their parents have remained stationary in that respect? Is it not highly probable, that in the course of a much longer life they may have traversed some path which has been hitherto unexplored by their families, or may have stumbled against something which has not yet lain in their children's way?

The best proof that can be given of our having attained some degree of wisdom and discretion, is a modest deference to the opinions of those who, in the natural order of things, may reasonably claim it. The young and the ignorant are prone to be self-opiniated and impatient of control, simply because they *are* young and ignorant, ignorant especially of *themselves.*

The revolutions made by time in the manners and customs of society, are sometimes urged by young people in excuse for their non-conformity to the opinions or wills of their seniors, which they are apt to deem out of date, and inapplicable to the modes and habits

of the present day; but it is presumed there
are no parents who require that the cut of
their children's clothes should conform to the
fashion of their own, when, years ago, they
were beaus and belles, at the height of the *ton*;
or who insist on constructing their chairs with
backs as high or as low as those on which
themselves could once repose at ease: but
although coats and cloaks, and chairs and
tables, assume new shapes with every passing
year, there are things in which the revolutions of time make no change; " as face
answereth to face in a glass, so does the heart
of man to man" in all ages and circumstances.
Parents and children can exist in no period
in which the former may not with propriety
caution the latter against pride, and vanity,
and dissipation, however the modes of gratifying those vices may vary.

It is an erroneous notion which the young
and thoughtless are apt to entertain, that ad-
vancing age is necessarily connected with
mental imbecility.*   In every stage of life

* " The soul's dark cottage, batter'd and decay'd,
  Lets in new light through chinks that time has made."

we frequently observe minds of no ordinary
character united with feeble and decrepit
frames: it therefore cannot follow, that bodily
vigour, and the powers of the understanding,
must necessarily decline together. Of the
Christian it is said, that " while his outward
man decays, his inward man is renewed day by
day." This, indeed, is effected by divine influence; yet there is nothing irrational in the
idea, (and it is confirmed by experience) that
the natural powers and faculties of the mind
are equally capable of improvement. Where
not obstructed by mental defect, and where
they are assisted by opportunities for observation, they *will* improve, and if accompanied by
rectitude of principle, will become of increasing value in the common conduct of life. It
is well for those young persons who view the
subject in this light, and avail themselves
of such needful assistance,—attending with
humble and unprejudiced minds to the admonitions of experienced age, to the wisdom of
accumulated years, although the full value
of such instructions may not appear till some
future, perhaps distant, emergency. Perchance,

the story twice told, had even better be thrice
repeated than not told at all : like many an in-
significant being on whom we are apt to look
with contempt, it may happen to render us
some unexpected service in a time of need.
" I remember my father used to observe,"
may be repeated with very different sensations
from what were felt at the time the observation was made. " My son, hear thou then the
instruction of thy father, and forsake not the
law of thy mother ; for they shall be ornaments of grace about thy head, and chains
of gold about thy neck."

But such influence will be most easily and
effectually attained by parents aiming at that
character and conduct, which ensures the
respect of their children. " I will walk before
mine house with a perfect heart," should be
the humble resolution of every one who sus-
tains this important relation. It should not
suffice that the character ranks high abroad,
while the family at home is constrained to
hold very different sentiments respecting it :
that applause is of little value which is not
echoed by the domestic circle. Children have

an early perception of right and wrong, and
will involuntarily learn to appreciate their
parents according to their merits. The disre-
spectful conduct of children should always
awaken an inquiry on the part of parents,
with regard to the origin of the evil : perhaps
it will appear after such an investigation, that
they have few claims to regard beyond those
of natural affection. In this case, an amend-
ment of their own conduct is the first step
towards reforming that of their children; for
he is incompetent to manage an unruly animal,
who cannot maintain his own balance, and
keep himself steady in his seat.

A ponderous task, indeed, they have, if
they must begin to practise the first rudiments
of mental discipline on themselves, at a period
when their families have become ungovernable; yet even this is not a hopeless case: a
sudden transition, indeed, cannot be expected;
the irritable will not become placid, the morose and sullen cheerful, the arbitrary and
tyrannical mild and gentle in a day; but if
once there is a conviction of the necessity
for improvement, and sufficient principle and

energy of mind to attempt it, much will be
effected:—the character will rise almost imperceptibly; that self-respect will be induced,
which stimulates to renewed efforts; and thus
a lesson would be afforded by the striking
example of a renovated character, much more
effectual than any (however well intended)
that can be suggested in these pages.

To those who question their strength,
and are tempted to exclaim, "How can *I*
recover the esteem of my family? Can *I* plant
the lily and the rose in a soil so long overgrown with thorny weeds? Can the Ethiopian
change his skin, or the leopard his spots?" it
must indeed be replied, " our sufficiency is
only of God." But this consideration affords
the highest encouragement to make the effort,
in His strength, who alone can render crooked
places straight, and rough places plain : He
has performed such wonders in every age, and
he will continue his operations to the end of
time. The Apostle Paul, after enumerating
a melancholy catalogue of offenders, adds,
" And such were some of you, but ye are
washed, but ye are sanctified in the name of

the Lord Jesus, and by the spirit of our God."
Where then is the strong hold which shall be
impervious to the same almighty power? Parents, especially, have the most urgent motives
for pleading earnestly at the throne of grace
for this renovating change, which shall influence their natural tempers and dispositions,
and shed an agreeable lustre over their whole
deportment. How vast the responsibility, if
on their own characters so greatly depend, as
a means, the spiritual as well as the temporal
interests of their offspring! When a principle of life is infused into the root, the
branches may be expected to bud, and in due
time to yield fruit. Let them resolve then,
in divine strength, and say, "As for me and
my house, we will serve the Lord."

The necessity for paying the strictest attention to our own characters, as the foundation
on which family virtue must be built, will
further appear, if we consider that in whatever
department we employ the services of others,
we require them to be competent to the task
they undertake. We make strict inquiry even
into the qualifications of our menial servants,

and either do not engage them, or dismiss
them when engaged, if they are not expert
and skilful at their proper business. Our
dwellings, our furniture, our food and cloth-
ing, must be the work of hands skilled in their
respective employments ; especially our infants
are entrusted with confidence to the care of a
nurse, accustomed to the management of children; and when it becomes necessary to
transfer them to other hands, tutors and
governesses are expected to be proficient in
whatever they undertake to teach. If so,
what manner of persons ought parents themselves to be, who have, or ought to have, the
superintendance of the whole,—on whom,
by right and duty, it devolves to lay the foundation of the structure, to assist in raising it,
and to place the top stone with their own
hands ? What manner of persons ought they
to be, on whose conduct and example the
future destinies of their posterity so essentially depend ? As they desire the respect of
their rising families, the momentous work before them should be the first object to engage
the deep attention of every couple at the very
commencement of their arduous duties. It is

not sufficient that the lady can make beautiful
baby-linen, nor that the gentleman can pay
charges; rather let them institute a rigid
inquiry into their own tempers and qualifications, for executing the great and difficult,
but honourable and " delightful task," of
training young minds to knowledge and virtue. " Can we," let them ask, " love our
children so much better than ourselves, as to
sacrifice our humours, our prejudices, our
vanity, our time, to their true interests? Let
not the attention of the mother be absorbed in
those petty externals, which may enable *her*
children to vie with those of her neighbours,
in dress and appearance, when they walk
abroad with their nurse-maids; let not the
father suppose he is fulfilling his whole duty,
and entitling himself to the future respect
of his family, while amassing property for
those who, if they follow his example,
will not know how to use it: but rather, by
unremitting observation and care, let each
party accumulate that appropriate stock of
wisdom and experience, which alone can obtain
the *respect* of their children, and will assuredly
prove of more intrinsic value to them, than

any inheritance which they may be enabled
to bequeath them.

Children, whose parents are truly qualified,
are highly privileged indeed. Let them manifest a grateful sense of their advantages, by
an affectionate and respectful deportment;
let them " give honour to whom honour is
so justly due." The value of a *good* education cannot be fully estimated by those who
are receiving it, the benefit extends so far;
it treasures up a stock of happiness, not only
for the individuals themselves, but for others
yet unborn. Yes, and the benefit of a good
education is unlimited in its influence,—it
extends to another state of existence.

Let not parents forget, that there is a
respect due to the *young*, as well as to the old.
It has a happy influence on the character when
this is judiciously yielded : it will make an
ingenuous spirit solicitous to deserve it, and
impel to praise-worthy actions. Are they
not deserving of it, if they have made advances
in wisdom and knowledge proportionate to
their years and opportunities? There is no
crime in the inexperience of youth, provided
it does not assume a consequence to which it

is not entitled ; nor should youth, or even
inexperience, ever be mentioned in terms of
contempt or reproach.

Were the above principles mutually acted
upon, they would produce the happiest effects
on domestic life : parents, worthy of respect,
would more frequently be respected by their
children ; while children, feeling a due return,
would more often endeavour to deserve it. Nor
would their juvenile attempts experience the
difficulties which their parents must encounter,
in the late and arduous work of self-renova-
tion : their advantages are greater, their ob-
stacles fewer, the motives are equally weighty
to impel them, and they have the promise of
the same divine assistance. As it is expressly
by their conduct at home that the character
of parents must be estimated, so it is of
little consequence in what repute their children
are held abroad, among their gay and thoughtless companions. The grand question is, have
their *fathers* and their *mothers* just occasion to approve and *respect* them ? This is
the best security for the permanent approbation of the wise and good. It is the dutiful
and respectful child, whom we must select

for the kind neighbour, and the warm and disinterested friend. As our family finds us *within*-doors, so society will find us *without*, sooner or later, with whatever superficial gloss we may for the present conceal our real characters. What happy effects, in all the departments of life, may not be fairly anticipated, from the *mutual respect* of parents and children!

CHAP. III.

FAMILY HARMONY.

" Behold, how good and how pleasant it is for brethren to dwell together in unity !"   PSALM cxxxiii. 1.

THERE are few readers, whether parents or
children, who need the aid of what has been
already suggested, to prove that domestic
happiness is in itself a most desirable object;
although it is not every one who is skilled in
the most effectual means for attaining it. Our
ears are not unfrequently assailed by the mutual complaints of parents and children:
what discordant and unnatural sounds !
Whence can they originate ?   Are the parties
new acquaintances, who have yet to learn
each other's tempers and dispositions ? This,
however strange it may seem, is sometimes
the case with children who are consigned

from the care of the nurse to that of the governess. Is it any wonder, if, when a young lady of sixteen returns to an almost strange home, there should not commence the most cordial understanding between herself and her mother ; though with what view their mutual discontents should be made public, it is not easy to conjecture. Parents! can you expose the foibles of your family, without exciting some suspicion of your own mismanagement? Children! can you undermine the reputation of your parents, without in a degree sapping your own ? *your father and your mother!* relatives, whose authority is protected by the divine sanction ; frail mortals like yourselves, entitled to have the mantle of love cast over them by the hands of filial affection, instead of being exposed to the condemnation or the ridicule of a censorious world.

It is often too apparent on what terms families live together, although they judiciously abstain from direct complaint or accusation, by the uncordial manner in which they speak to, or of each other, leaving us to conjecture, if we please, that things are in reality worse than they appear. If the good opinion

c

of society be of any value, this is not the direct method to obtain it. Neither party, as
they value the family respectability, should
address the other in the presence of by-standers but, at least, in terms of politeness and
respect.

Those who are in perfect harmony at
home, will most probably be so with their
neighbours; as they carry no complaints
abroad, they will seldom be annoyed by tales
brought home to them of the misconduct of
any of their happy groupe: should this ever
occasionally happen, parents will hear with
candour, and bear with patience, such com-
munications, nor resent as a mortal injury a
friendly hint, which, if properly received,
might prove eventually advantageous; they
will not be so weak as to imagine, that *their*
children must of course appear faultless
abroad, and be universally approved and
admired. Such persons, however, are apt
to make no scruple of doing that themselves,
which they so highly resent in their neighbours.

The ill-conduct of children may sometimes
be traced to the terms on which their parents

live together : nothing can operate more unfavourably on the disposition, than being accustomed to witness daily bickerings and altercations; to say nothing of that open hostility which must, of course, be destructive of all that is amiable. Would parents who really love their children, and have their happiness at heart, give due weight to these considerations, it would suppress many a useless dispute, and conduce much to the tranquillity of the fire-side. If it be desirable to render the morning of life tranquil and serene, from the anticipation of mid-day storms, this would contribute greatly towards it. Fathers and mothers who would ensure the love and esteem of their children, must let it appear that they esteem and love each other. How little self-denial do those parents exercise, who cannot refrain from petty disputes and contradictions in the presence of their families, who consequently acquire the like wretched habits of discord among themselves. We can by no means be sure that children will follow a *good* example, but their imitating a *bad* one may be calculated upon almost with certainty It is still worse to make them

parties in such affairs, however trivial they
may be. Should a tormented husband or an
oppressed wife need filial consolation, it
must be remembered, that nothing short of a
very judicious education can render the
bosom of a child a fit receptacle for connubial grievances. A young person should be
possessed of much prudence, and delicacy, and
affection, to be confided with the failings of
that being, whom he is bound by ties, human
and divine, to love and honour. At all events,
let the moral infirmities of *fathers* and *mothers*,
when they cannot be concealed, be only
called into requisition for the benefit of *sons*
and *daughters*, against a time when they
may assume those important relations themselves. A discreet and affectionate parent
will endeavour to steer his family clear
from the rocks on which his own vessel has
foundered.

Children whose unhappy lot it is to witness domestic dissensions, are certainly in a
difficult, as well as in an irksome situation;
they can scarcely espouse the cause of one
parent, without failing in proper respect to
the other. Even in trifling disputes, there is

a delicacy to be observed which would well
become them : they should either remain
silent, or if obliged to advance an opinion,
and take a part, it should be in such a way
as can give no reasonable offence. An affectionate temper and conciliating manners,
united with a little address, may sometimes
extinguish a spark, which unheeded, neglected, or urged, might produce a serious con-
flagration. Debates which augur an unpleasant
termination, might frequently be diverted by
the adroit introduction of some subject foreign
to the matter in hand. It is a happy circumstance, when young people have sufficient
inclination and address, to do this without
apparent design; to change the subject on
which they perceive their parents *cannot*
agree, to one on which they are sure they
will. "A word spoken in due season how good
is it!" We hope it would be an unnecessary
digression to address the *family incendiary :*
should, however, such an eye glance at these
pages, will not those engaging terms, filial
love, connubial affection, domestic felicity,
and all the soft and harmonious sounds
which are so gratifying to the virtuous ear,

be totally unintelligible to it? totally unaffecting to one who has arrived at this advanced stage of domestic crime? *A family incendiary!* Should conscience accuse any of meriting such a harsh epithet, let them pause, at least for their own sakes, and consider the probable consequences of this conduct. Can we jar the pillars on which the building rests but at our own peril?—" A house divided against itself cannot stand ;"—cannot stand to answer the desirable purposes of a domestic establishment : and those who attempt to divide it, must in some degree participate in its overthrow. " Where no wood is, the fire goeth out : so where there is no tale-bearer, the strife ceaseth."

O let not children mar the peace of one parent, and the character of the other, by any malevolent suggestions of theirs; rather should they stand in the breach, and endeavour to answer one of the purposes for which Providence designed them : rather let them be links in the chain, to bind those together whom God has joined, and who should be separated by no man, much less by their own offspring.

But let not afflicted parents seek consolation in vain in the filial bosom. Let them be *comforted*, not *irritated;* nor be obliged, for want of sympathy at home, to carry their grievances abroad, or to brood alone under their sorrows,—a species of suffering which the human mind can rarely sustain.

But to return to parents, to whom this part of the subject is more exclusively addressed; let it be observed, that the future prospects of that family are very unenviable who have lived in habitual discord : strangers to domestic peace, they will not be skilful in promoting it wherever they may go, nor be solicitous to plant a tree whose fruits they have never tasted. Probably it will not suffice them to have repaid the humours of their parents by obstinacy and rebellion, but they may retaliate the sufferings of their early days on the heads of children yet unborn; and their future families may reap the bitter fruits of those unhappy dissensions which now disgrace the domestic circle.

Perhaps your children will shortly quit the paternal roof, and enter on the busy scenes of life with principles and habits ill

adapted to promote their own happiness or
that of others; in that case, the remaining
opportunities are comparatively few in which
they can derive benefit either from paternal
precept or example : or should they remain
at home, you must shortly quit it; every passing year reiterates this warning, " set thine
house in order" by aiming at that general
excellence, which can only result from the
religion of Jesus. True religion furnishes its
possessors with arguments the most numerous, weighty, and solid, for the preservation
of domestic peace. " Peace on earth, and
good-will towards men," was one of the first
messages promulgated by the Gospel. So far
as its divine precepts gain access to the heart,
they will be apparent in the life, and prove
blessings to the house, as well as to the
church; for they are as essential to the private and individual Christian, as to the great
body of which he is a member.

It is true, that conduct the most circum-
spect cannot always ensure domestic felicity :
unerring Wisdom has warned us, that in the
world we shall have tribulation; but un-
changeable Love has bid us be of good cheer

notwithstanding, because our divine leader
has overcome the world. When we can take
this comfort, it is that we prove the value of
religion. Then we say, " Though my house
be not so with God, yet hath he made with me
an everlasting covenant, ordered in all things
and sure; this is all my salvation, and all my
desire." A Christian parent under the various trials peculiar to his relation, can yet say
in the darkest hour, " What am I, and what is
my house, that thou hast brought me hitherto ?" That thou hast given me such consolations, and afforded me such hopes? For
" thou hast spoken of thy servant for a great
while to come ;" and shall I expect also to
find in this wilderness some unexplored path,
decorated with perpetual verdure, and where
neither briars nor thorns infest the ground?
Shall showers of sorrows fall around me, and
shall I, like Gideon's fleece, remain secure and
dry? Have *I* maintained such an uninterrupted rectitude of conduct in all my relations, as to be authorised to expect no breach
of duty should occur towards myself? Rather
can I, " a living man, complain,—a man for
the punishment of his sins ?" O here is not

my rest!—it is polluted—I have helped to pollute it. " I am a pilgrim and a stranger, as all my fathers were. I travel towards a better country; and I will employ all the means with which, as a parent, Providence has invested me, to conduct my family into the same path,—to point them to the same goal.

CHAPTER IV.

SELF-WILL.

" And in their self-will they digged down a wall."

GENESIS, xlix. 6.

ALTHOUGH it is true that an enlightened system of education has done much, and it is hoped will do still more in restraining the violent and obvious actings of *self-will;* yet, experience, no less than revelation, proves the inefficiency of the most perfect system of human discipline, to *eradicate* any one of the diseases of our depraved nature. Besides, improvements of any kind make slow progress among the middling classes of society; because, only the well-informed and intelligent are capable of estimating their value. A few remarks on the subject may not therefore be inapplicable.

There is no passion of the human mind which manifests itself earlier, or which it requires more skill or firmness to control, than *self-will*. We have to encounter it in our children from their infancy; but there are many parents who do not perceive the necessity of opposing these early indications of it till it is too late: and those young persons, who are now experiencing in their own ungoverned tempers the sad effects of such mistaken tenderness, will, it is hoped, suffer the word of exhortation.

If the young feel it so very irksome to submit to the will of those who have a natural right to control them, how repugnant must it be to the feelings of parents to have the order of things reversed, and to live in subjection to their children! Do young people intend that their love of sway should *decrease* with their years? Do they indeed propose, when they become parents themselves, to relinquish quietly the reins of government into younger hands, and thus, in turn, submit to subjection? This, surely, is by no means their present intention, whatever may be the result: they may, however, at some future

time, be qualified from their own experience,
to form a just estimate of the sacrifices they
now exact. Does the seat of government
seem so very easy, that children are impatient
to occupy it?—Are those who covet the privilege, willing to pay the price? Would
they with the power, endure the burdens,
groan under the anxieties, partake the shat-
tered constitutions, the increasing infirmities
of their parents? It is hardly fair to desire
one without the other. Were these malcon-
tents left to themselves, they imagine they
could transform their present home into a
delectable paradise; but this is not permitted
them, and it is well for others, and especially
for *themselves*, that it is not. The superior
knowledge and capacity of children to their
parents should certainly be first ascertained,
ere such arbitrary and unnatural reverses are
attempted. They should be able to prove
undeniably, that at the age of sixteen, or
twenty, while their contemporaries have been
amused with the trifles of childhood, the frivolities of youth, or at most have been but
preparing themselves for the approaching
duties of life; they have made so rapid a pro-

gress in the knowledge of men and things, as
to qualify them for the general superintendance of affairs, and to warrant them in placing
their *Fathers* and their *Mothers* in the back
ground, and rendering them ciphers in their
own houses! They must have been greatly
at a loss before their children became wise
enough thus to direct them!

But the good sense of the reader will revolt at these suppositions; while, should there
be any, who from mere thoughtlessness, may
in some degree have authorised them, they
will modestly retire into their proper places,
and there abide until the time arrives, when
nature and Providence shall summon them to
more arduous duties.

We never appear to advantage but when
we act in character, when we cheerfully conform to the situation in which we are placed.
That modesty, humility, and diffidence are
peculiarly appropriate to the young, the general suffrages of mankind sufficiently testify.
These virtues ensure love and approbation
wherever they are found; while obstinacy
and positiveness, and that spirit of contradic-
tion which is their almost inseparable com-

panion, produce corresponding effects, and keep such unhappy tempers in a state of perpetual warfare with all around. A tenaciousness of opinion, the result of a vain self-complacency, is an unequivocal symptom of ignorance. Genuine wisdom, founded on experience, is seldom positive: with a true dignity, it leaves the self-conceited to the enjoyment of opinions which, indeed, are rarely worth contending for.

There is not a greater, nor a more unhappy mistake, than that of imagining we are sent into the world to *have our own way:* our humours, and passions, and propensities must be thwarted in the very nature of things, in a world where there is such a diversity of tempers, and so much clashing of interests. No sooner does the human being begin to discern objects, than it grasps and cries to possess all it beholds; but some it would destroy, some would prove destructive to itself, and some are the property of others, with whose rights it is as yet unacquainted: as it increases in knowledge, the objects are changed, but the propensity remains; and it is well when parental discipline co-operates with an over-rul-

ing Providence, to curb those exorbitant
desires; well, especially, when the subject is
enabled to discern the hand from whence, and
the reason why he is crossed in his pursuits;
he will then become patient, submissive, and
thoughtful: but when, regardless of such
wholesome discipline, the mind revolts from
instruction, and when self-gratification continues to be the primary object, mortification
and chagrin await it at every turn. He has
commenced a warfare with his fellow-creatures, in which he must eventually be van-
quished. God and man unite to thwart
his unwarrantable, and to frustrate his vain
hopes.

But there are errors in the temper and
conduct, which, while they assume a less for-
midable aspect than ungoverned *self-will*,
have, perhaps, as great a tendency to destroy
domestic happiness. *Peevishness* and discon-
tent are faults, which many an indulgent (too
indulgent) parent has to lament, who cannot,
perhaps, complain of open rebellion in his
children; but might not such ungracious
tempers be more frequently counteracted, if
young persons would but consider that the

sun which is *rising* on their own hemisphere, is *setting* in that of their parents? Is it not desirable that the *evening* of their days, at least, should be tranquil and serene? After enduring the heat and burden of the day, nature requires repose; and if the grasshopper be a burden, a dutiful child will assiduously chase it away. There are those who at the hazard of their lives would rescue their parents from the fire, or the water, or from any other imminent danger which might threaten; who yet, when it is but a straw that incommodes them, will not give themselves the trouble to remove it! But that filial attachment which never manifests itself but upon such urgent occasions, is of a doubtful nature, and will not, it is to be feared, bear investigation.

Children who are conscious of irregularities in their own temper, may well make some allowance for those of their parents, who have at present so much more to try them; they ought also to take heed, lest what they feel to be so troublesome and oppressive in the conduct of others, should attach to their own. Indeed the best, and almost the only

use we can make of observing the faults of
our fellow-creatures, is to guard against the
same in ourselves.

Children were originally intended by an
indulgent Providence as *blessings;* accordingly they are styled " an heritage of the
Lord," and bestowed as one of the most
precious of temporal gifts : but those who by
their untoward conduct prove thorns in the
sides of their parents, cruelly pervert these
gracious designs, and manifest a spirit of im-
piety truly offensive to God. There is an
indefinite carriage and conduct in some young
persons towards their parents, which, although
not decidedly hostile, is sufficient to deter
a by-stander from coveting *such* an heritage.
Something rather in the *manner* than the
matter which marks their usual communica-
tions with them, as though they were address-
ing beings, not merely of different ages and
circumstances, but of a different species from
themselves, with whom they could have no
sympathetic feelings whatever; while they
intrench themselves in expressions which, if
repeated, would appear, perhaps, perfectly
unexceptionable, and afford no plausible reason for complaint.

Parental love, however, is not easily shaken; it remains proof against great irregularities of temper, and will often endure all that youthful caprice and thoughtlessness so ungratefully or so carelessly inflict : but woe to the child, whose irritating conduct occasions the continual displeasure excited in the parental bosom to settle into a fixed disapprobation! A parent may thereby inflict what is remote from his heart, and entail an involuntary *curse* upon one, on whose head every blessing would be still implored. *A parent's blessing! A parent's curse!* Did children duly consider how prophetic these frequently prove, and that what is thus uttered on earth, may by a just and retributive Providence be ratified in heaven, and become an immutable decree, they would not think lightly of either.

But *self-will*, and the various bad passions and evil propensities which originate in that fruitful source, are not, alas! always confined to the younger branches of a family. Let not parents then who possess so many advantages from their age and experience, from the knowledge they ought to have of themselves,

as well as of others, for detecting and resisting their faults, be remiss and negligent with
their own characters in this respect : the faults
of maturity are more harsh and offensive, as
well as more inexcusable, than those of youth.
Self-will in a parent is *tyranny:* the obedience it exacts from the family is not that of
sons, but of slaves. Some persons under the
idea of maintaining parental authority, which
they deem the grand art of education, assume
the character rather of the master than of the
father : human nature is equally prone to
love power, and to abuse it ; those who are
intrusted with it, should be constantly aware
of this tendency. Let fathers and mothers
often recur to their own youthful days, with
all the desires, aversions, propensities, and
levities which characterised them. Such recollections might go far towards rendering their
requisitions reasonable and considerate. With
them, these youthful ebullitions have subsided,
and perhaps the revolution in their manners
and feelings is as much the result of care and
sorrow as of years. They have reason then to
anticipate the same impressive lessons for
their children ; for " man is born to trouble."

A considerate father, therefore, when he sur-
veys the wilderness in which he has been long
travelling, and sees his children just commencing their journey through it, will be
solicitous to strew a few flowers over a path
which may decrease in verdure at every step.
It would be well for both parents and
children, if the following anecdote had the
charm of novelty to recommend it; but although similar occurrences are within every
one's recollection, so as perhaps to render the
relation uninteresting, and certainly common-
place; yet it is not every one who has made
a judicious application of such events to their
own circumstances.

The two Miss W.'s were the only children
of their fond parents, who so far from check-
ing or discouraging the early indications of
self-will which they manifested, were exceedingly amused by them, and thought, that in
their children, at least, they were peculiarly
engaging; constantly palliating any action
which required a decided apology, by saying
" they would know better by and by." They
were deemed too young to be controlled, till
control was unavailing; till what had hereto-

fore been very interesting, became very troublesome ; and would have been insupportable
but for the prospect of complete renovation
under boarding-school discipline. The parents imagined (as many do) that there the
whole process of education commences and
terminates ; and while the management of
two individuals in whom they were so deeply
interested was deemed by themselves imprac-
ticable, they formed the most sanguine expectations from the efforts of one who had twenty
or thirty under her superintendance ! Vain
hopes ! as if the right formation of the human
mind could be effected by a mechanical process ! as if education were like the military
evolutions of the field ! as if virtue and intelligence might be brought into action at the
word of command ! The flattering aspect of
the line, so compact and trim ; the pointed
steel and gaudy feather, motionless through
all the ranks, till animated by a word, or the
note of a bugle, must by no means be taken as
any indication of the orderly dispositions and
regular manners of the individuals who make
up the show. With as little certainty can we
conclude, from the external order produced

in seminaries, that the mind and heart are
trained in them to virtue and goodness.

Parents who have imagined that schools
could do every thing, have afterwards, from
their own bitter experience, as hastily con-
cluded that they could do nothing. Such at
least was the opinion of poor Mr. and Mrs.
W. when after years of unlimited expense,
their *finished* daughters returned home, having as they imagined, learned every thing—
of course, there was nothing more to learn :
as they were no longer children, but young
women, they were competent to govern themselves, and by a very slight advance of authority, they conceived that they were qualified
to govern their parents also. Under such circumstances, the situation in which *they* now
found themselves may be well conceived :
they lost all authority in their own house, and
were really under greater subjection than any
of their servants. The consoling hope of their
children's " knowing better by and by" had
been long discarded ; that prospect, at least,
appeared too distant to afford much encouragement. Nor did the terms on which the
young ladies lived with each other, contribute

at all to *family harmony*. " I wish," said Mrs.
W. to her husband, " that Charlotte and
Sarah were well married." " I wish so to,"
replied he, " if *well* married." " It was a pity
they had not continued longer at school," observed she. " I don't see how that would have
answered any good purpose," said he ; " they
were ruined before they went ; but wishes are
vain now." " I don't know," said she, " what
we could have done better, they always had
such high spirits, as to be quite unmanageable." " And yet," said he, " some people
have the art of managing such spirits, but it
was never our *forte*." Mrs. W. sighed, and
the conversation ended.

The former part of the wish, however,
was shortly realized : the young ladies received the overtures of two lovers nearly at the
same time, which, as they neither of them
met with the approbation of either father or
mother, would have been rejected had their
opinion been consulted : but parents who
were not allowed to arrange the affairs of
their own household, could have little influence in the choice of their daughter's husbands ; so they made a virtue of necessity, by

giving a reluctant consent; and solaced themselves in the prospect of their own emancipa
tion from the daily vexations under which
they groaned, which was all of comfort that
appeared to remain. These, however, were
fallacious hopes : the eldest daughter having
married a *kindred soul,* was soon embroiled
with her husband, and again assailed the
peace of her still fond parents with her domestic quarrels ;—while the husband of the
younger having squandered all her dowry
(though, to do him justice, she had her full
share in the dissipation of it), left her with
three children in indigence; with these, who
inherited no small portion of their mother's
spirit, she sought an asylum in her father's
house. With an income materially decreased
by the misfortunes and imprudence of their
children, they had now in the decline of life
an increase of family, with all the multiplied
vexations arising from ungovernable tempers
and perverse dispositions. Adversity had rendered their daughter *irritable,* but not humble;
while their own spirits were broken by the
accumulation of family disasters.

The father's afternoon naps were generally

interrupted by the noise and clamour of three unmanageable children, whom their mother would not endure to have controlled, and who had rather that her father should be disturbed than that her children should cry. From these troubles Mrs. W. was soon released: her enfeebled frame sunk under the effects of accumulated vexation and fatigue. With what sensations she left her aged husband to the care of such a family may be easily conceived.

Let those who would avoid similar calamities, be solicitous to detect first in themselves, and then in their children, the earliest indication of *self-will.*

CHAPTER IV.

ON SOME MISTAKES IN EDUCATION, AND THE CORRECTION OF THEM.

" Whatsoever a man soweth, that shall he also reap."

THAT a great proportion of the ill conduct which destroys the peace of families originates in *mistakes in education*, there can be little doubt; it may not, therefore, be amiss, before we proceed upon other subjects, to point out a few of them; for to enumerate the whole would occupy too large a portion of these pages.

Not to direct our first assault against that principle of *selfishness* to which in many families such costly sacrifices are made, would be like lopping the branches of a noxious tree,

and leaving the root in the ground; some
parents do not discern, that in proportion as
this principle is cherished, they are producing
consequences directly opposite to their designs. It has never occurred to them with
any salutary conviction (although their own
experience might have enforced the lesson),
that the majority of mankind has adopted
each for himself this identical idol,—dearer,
more interesting to the individual, than was
" great Diana of the Ephesians" to her wor-
shippers.—Ah! no wonder then there are
such clamours without doors and within ! "—
No wonder if the voice of any one in particular, however vociferous, be lost in the general din, " *great is myself;*" " to *my* honour,
my pleasure, *my* caprice, shall be sacrificed the
feelings and the interests of all around me ! "—
Until, however, this domineering principle is
subdued, the human character cannot be con-
templated with complacency; nor till we are
brought to comply with the divine precepts
of the Gospel, which direct us to esteem
others above ourselves, can we experience
true peace of mind and inward tranquillity.
How would such holy principles, early im-

planted in the young mind, sap the foundation of all those moral evils which torment
and harrass mankind! To which of them
would they not prove destructive, an appropriate, an efficient cure ?

With what an egregious mistake are those
parents chargeable, who foster in their children the spirit of party, of bigotry, and of in-
tolerance! *Their* notions, *their* party, *their*
sect (as if the world and their own depraved
nature did not furnish them with materials
enough) must be put in requisition to complete the character, and stamp it altogether un-
amiable. How disgusting to hear a little bigot,
or party-man, prating about who he is *for,*
and who he is against; although he knows not
why, or wherefore! Yet this intolerant spirit
has sometimes found its way into public seminaries, and occasioned the most disgraceful
divisions. Is this the method parents take to
promote their children's happiness, or the
public weal? Do they forget that God is love,
and that his express command is, that we love
one another? It is not from such discordant
materials as these that the true citizen, the
true patriot, and what is still more, the true

Christian, can be formed. He is actuated by principles of universal philanthropy : the divine precepts of the Gospel, which are the rule of his conduct, are in direct opposition to such a temper. " Not," as Dr. Watts observes, " that it is at all amiss in parents to train up their children in their own forms of worship, at least so far as any of their peculiar opinions enter into their forms of public religion." It is hardly possible to avoid this, for religion cannot be practised but it must be in some particular mode; therefore children must be educated in some forms, and opinions, and modes of worship; and it is the duty of parents to educate them in those ways which they think nearest the truth, and most pleasing to God. But all that I mean here is this, that as I would not have these particulars of different sects to enter into the public practice of religion further than is needful; so it should be far the greatest care and solicitude of parents to teach their children christianity itself, rather than the particular and distinguishing tenets of sects and parties.

But the errors of this unthinking class of parents are innumerable; when they have by

erroneous principles planted, or by neglect
suffered, and by every species of pampering
and indulgence firmly rooted and nourished the *selfish* principle in their children during
infancy and childhood, it is no uncommon
case when (as a natural consequence) they
begin themselves to reap the bitter fruits of
it, for them to attempt to rectify one mistake
by another equally mischievous, by substi-
tuting ill-timed severity for excessive indulgence.   We have sometimes observed with
grief how the fawning tones of these injudicious parents have in a few years degenerated
into the harsh sounds of perpetual chiding,
or unreasonable peevishness.   Is it a wonder
if the unhappy subjects of such unprincipled
discipline should pursue any road but the
right, when they have no skilful hand to
guide them into it, but are driven about at
random, just according to the impulse of the
present moment?

Parents are frequently disposed to magnify
the natural sagacity and acuteness of their
children; they are forward to discover indications of superior genius or talent in them:
their wonderful remarks and achievements

are deemed worthy to be exhibited and repeated before all companies! Should it not
previously be ascertained, that the same
things repeated or done by their neighbour's
children would appear equally interesting and
extraordinary ?—It is granted, however, that
some allowance should be made to a fond parent on this subject; and every fond parent
is qualified to make it, and to sympathize in
such feelings under proper restrictions; but
we would still add a caution against extremes,
lest what is so interesting to parents, should
appear ridiculous, or become irksome to
friends.   Children should seldom be required
to repeat by rote before company, unless indeed it be some pious hymn or song to their
minister, or to a christian friend who may be
supposed to take an interest in their improvement. Such customs are apt to generate conceit and confidence in children, while they
afford little gratification to their hearers.
People, in general, much prefer uttering
their own extempore effusions, to sitting mute
while a school-boy spouts forth a long poem
by rote. It certainly adds nothing to his credit in the estimation of the intelligent part of

his audience; for he must be an incorrigible
dunce, indeed, who cannot acquire such an
art as this. Although we have seen a doating grandmother, who, if the expression of
her countenance might be trusted, plainly in-
dicated that she attached all the merit of
Gray's Elegy to the lad who was repeat-
ing it!

Much less when a child displays such unequivocal talents as surrounding friends are
constrained to admit, and willing to admire,
should he be brought forward for public exhibi-
tion: nothing can be more inimical to the
sterling worth of his character.—It is well if
such a child does not become insufferably pert
and disagreeable; well, indeed, if those unpleasant qualities do not in time degenerate
into what is worse. We have seen a child of
this description introduced to a numerous
company, with a confident look and air ill
becoming his age. Secure of admiration, he
was under no restraint; while even his non-
sense was applauded, as something extraordinary. " O parents! parents!" thought some
who were present, " it will be well if one day
you do not dearly pay for your vanity."

" Well, but *my* child," says many a
fond parent, " *is* unquestionably clever."—
Indeed!—Then you see your work before
you; it is cut out ready to your hand; although the framing and putting it together
may prove a more difficult task than you are
aware of: should you perform it negligently
or unskilfully, it were better that your labour
had been bestowed on more homely materials.
A genius neglected or mismanaged is ever
to be deplored.—A rich soil unfruitful or
overgrown with weeds, must reflect disgrace
and bring misfortune on the husbandman.
Double your diligence then, otherwise those
talents which were originally dispensed as
blessings, will ultimately prove the very reverse, to society, to yourselves, and to the
being on whom they are bestowed.

On the other hand, if there be evil in the
conduct from too great partiality or indulgence, there may be also in injudicious restraint and violent coercion: there are parents
who do not distinguish between *curbing* the
spirits of children and *breaking* them; who
do not consider that the subjects of this process are in danger of degenerating either into

meanness and imbecility of character, or into
low cunning and hypocrisy, equally unfriend-
ly to the right performance of duty. Considerate parents will proportion their expressions
of disapprobation to youthful levities, or more
deeply-rooted faults.

It is true their wisdom and patience are
sometimes put to severe proof by the variety
of tempers they have to encounter, the discipline for one being, perhaps, quite opposite to
that which is suitable for another : they are
constrained in a sense to adopt the apostle's
conduct, who was willing to become all things
to all men for the general good.—A *mild* system is, however, always to be preferred, if
possible : yet it must be *firm ;* not a firmness
resulting from obstinacy or caprice, but from
sound principle, and mature judgment. The
young reader then will excuse it, when it is
repeated that it should be *firm.* That parents
must bear rule in their own houses, should
be as extensively published as the decree of
Ahasuerus, and remain as irrevocable as the
laws of the Medes and Persians. Let those
who feel inclined to relax their discipline, or
to submit for the sake of present quiet to the

obstinacy or clamour of their children, younger or elder, be admonished not to yield what
is right, just, and prudent—no, not for an
hour: that hour's peace may be purchased
with years of anarchy and sorrow. Their mental powers and their just authority in their
own houses should only expire together.

Yet it should be conceded, that although
it is the duty as well as the right of parents
to rule and direct their children, and to order
their own concerns in all essential matters,
there are subjects on which the young may
be better informed than themselves, cases in
which they may be allowed, in a certain sense,
to dictate to their parents, who may listen to
their suggestions without at all endangering
parental authority, or derogating from the
wisdom of age. They have, in some instances,
more general intercourse with the world than
their parents now have, and, probably, they
feel a more lively interest in what passes
there: this may produce a quicker discern-
ment on various subjects of minor importance,
which may be as well conceded to them.
There is no virtue in wearing the habit,
speaking the language, or persevering in the

customs of fifty years ago. The period of
half a century does not necessarily render
things worse, as some elderly persons are apt
to assert, any more than that it must universally improve them, as the young so pertina-
ciously maintain.

And now, while some young readers may
be disposed to take advantage of the preceding remarks, and complain of their scanty
privileges, others, not feeling things quite as
they ought to be with themselves, may be
willing enough to lay all the blame on their
parents, to charge the whole on their bad
management, and to say, " Had I been differently educated, I should have proved a
better character; but the habits I have contracted are now become so firmly rooted, as
to be, I fear, beyond my power of control."
This may be too true; but I beseech you make
the same allowance for your parents, who
had, probably, equal disadvantages to deplore: nay, it may be fairly presumed, that
they were still greater; for the system of education is so much improved since their early
days, that it is probable even your opportunities have been superior to theirs.   Per-

haps they have acquitted themselves to you to the best of their knowledge and ability : they might even, while sowing the seeds of some of those faults in your temper, of which you cannot but be conscious, imagine that they were actually educating you well. If when you behaved amiss, they threatened to send you to bed, or to school; if they shut you in the dark, or called the old man, or the harmless cat or dog, to frighten you ; or if your good conduct was rewarded with cakes or sugar-plums, fine hats or frocks, thereby so enslaving you to sensual gratifications and groundless fears, as to produce much present misery, and threaten still more to yourself and others ; yet your happiness was the grand end they aimed at in all they did, although they miserably mistook the means. Gratitude for their zeal, though mistaken, is a debt you should ever acknowledge.

But should the conviction of former errors at length force itself upon them, should they endeavour to rectify their former mistakes by more judicious discipline in future, will you submit to it *now* ? Will you endure to be told of your faults, and suffer reproof

without resentment and impatience? Will
you bear denial of any of your accustomed
gratifications, or apply yourself to the performance of any difficult or painful duty which
is repugnant to your feelings, or contrary to
your present habits? Will you begin to be
tractable and humble, co-operating with them
in endeavouring to rectify past errors? It is
not too làte to do this; not too late to make
the attempt, even without their assistance.
Your increasing years and opening prospects,
whatever they may be, call most forcibly for
such renovating energies, otherwise your own
family, should Providence decree you to have
one, will be in the very predicament which
you now deplore. Commence your operations then ere the cares and anxieties of life
assail you, that you may be the more effectually qualified to encounter them. There is
much to *undo*, as well as *do*; your leisure days
are, perhaps, nearly expired: employ them
not in unavailing, and indeed unbecoming
complaints against the conduct of those who
may possibly have done their best by you;
but in endeavouring to amend your own,
especially if you are convinced that you have

not in all respects done the best by yourself, or acted according to the knowledge you possessed.

If the *selfish* principle has been instilled into you, by whatever means, against that, as was before observed, the first assault must be directed : however you may have been admired and extolled by your parents or by others, or whatever confidence or self-satisfaction you may have felt, if you will but take the trouble to investigate your own character with impartiality, with the secret motions and actings of your own heart, you will find enough to humble you, and to level your self-complacency with the dust. If this is a work, my young friend, to which you have been hitherto unaccustomed, and the process is utterly strange to you, bring your *whole self* to the standard of Scripture, your most secret thoughts, as well as your words and actions : this is the only way to produce that genuine humility which must be the basis of all other virtues—which is the only foundation of the christian character. Remember, that he only who humbleth himself shall be exalted : and this is true in a moral as well

as in a scriptural sense; for it is not those
who are so desirous of the uppermost seats,
who find their neighbours equally ready to
give place to them. The principle of humility in its universal extent, while it places you
at the feet of those of your fellow-creatures
who are qualified to instruct, will also conduct you to the foot of the cross as one destitute and helpless, weak and ignorant. This
it is to be a *Christian*; and when you are a
Christian, and not before, we may reasonably
expect you to acquit yourself well in all the
relations of life.

CHAP. V.

PECUNIARY AFFAIRS.

" It is the fate of almost every passion, when it has
passed the bounds which nature prescribes, to counteract
its own purposes."   RAMBLER.

THERE is no subject which produces more
frequent altercations in families than pecuniary affairs : a tendency to parsimony on one
side, and to prodigality on the other, cannot
but occasion disputes between parents and
children. A love of profusion either evidences
much inexperience, or it proves that even experience has failed to produce its proper
effect. They who are incessantly draining
their parents of money to defray super-
fluous expenses, have not yet considered how
easily property is dissipated by imperceptible
degrees : they have not been in the habit of
calculating for the future, and have no
thought beyond present gratification. It is

the attribute of prudence to " foresee the evil,
while the simple pass on and are punished."
To be indifferent to our future prospects, is
folly; to sacrifice the interests of near relatives to personal gratification, is selfish and
cruel: while children, perhaps, have no ap-
prehension that they are doing so, their
parents may have well-grounded fears on the
subject, quite sufficient to account for their
remonstrances and their resistance.

That an expensive style of dress is one of
the principal drains of property among our
own sex, needs not to be proved: much is it
to the disgrace of the matronly character,
that mothers are frequently no less eager
than their daughters to gratify this idle passion: and what is ultimately gained by indulging it? In what higher estimation do
dressy women stand with the wise and good,
with those whose opinions are of value?
Taste may harmonise the colours and adjust
the drapery, and symmetry of form may display the whole to advantage, while the mind
does not perhaps at all correspond with the
external appearance: there may exist neither
symmetry nor harmony there,—its scanty

furniture too plainly indicating that it has
occupied by far the least proportion of attention. While the outside show might gain
admittance into the gayest circles, the mind
may have been so far neglected as to be
utterly unfit for the society of the cultivated,
the polite, and. the better informed of either
sex; and still less qualified to find resources
in itself in the hours of solitude and retire-
ment, in the absence of a vain and alluring
world.

Of such characters it might be justly
inquired, "Wherefore will ye spend your
money for that which is not bread, and your
labour for that which satisfieth not?" What
rational mind but must deplore the accumulated mischiefs of this fatal propensity? Shall
it not be for a lamentation? In numberless
instances it has prevented its fair victims from
attaining those useful acquirements which
their extravagance has rendered doubly necessary in future life. Nor can this be a solitary
passion; it brings up many similar evils in
its train, all equally inimical to sterling excellence of character and to happiness; for upon
such persons Providence does not eventually

smile : of trivial and unworthy objects, pursued to excess, their votaries will one day have
to exclaim, " All is vanity and vexation of
spirit." Even in present gratifications of this
nature there is much alloy—a worm nibbling
at the root of the very choicest of them : and
it will be well if every sigh fetched from the
bosom of a parent by unreasonable exactions,
be not repaid by a briny tear, wrung either
from painful recollections, or from the pressure of present misfortunes.

It is hoped, however, that to many young
readers such remonstrances are not applicable ; or that where there exists an inclination
to unnecessary expense, a reasonable expostu-
lation will be sufficient to restrain it. Let
every one aim at a wise medium. The very
few persons who pass the other extreme, and
become careless of external appearances, betray
an equal error of judgment : a decent con-
formity to our circumstances, and to the society with which we rank, is neither unreasonable nor dangerous.

It must, however, be acknowledged that
children are not always chargeable with the
whole blame of domestic disputes even on

this subject; some of them have to endure
severe trials, from the unreasonable parsimony
of their parents : and where this is the case, it
has a hopeless aspect, because covetousness is
a vice rarely indeed extirpated in advanced
life. An appeal to the reason, to the feelings,
or even to the experience of the money-loving
is fruitless.

The discord produced among the nearest
relatives by the love of money, proves it to be
indeed " the root of all evil."

> " Gold begets in brothers hate,
> Gold in families debate."

Many whose feelings would revolt at those
heathen parents who used to sacrifice their
offspring to idols, make some advances towards
the crime they condemn, when their fondness
for gold impels them to sacrifice to it the happiness of those dependent on them: for
" covetousness is idolatry." To withhold
the means of enjoying those advantages in
society which belong to their circumstances
and their age, is unjust and cruel. Let it be
repeated—*the morning of life should be held
saered by parents,* as well as the evening of it

by their children. To youth many things are very requisite, which to forgetful age may not appear so. To ascertain what are the just claims of others upon us, it is always requisite to imagine ourselves in their circumstances, and they in ours. It is only by so doing that the golden rule of duty to our neighbour can be applied : what a surprising change would take place in some families, if this simple process were suddenly to commence ! But this is an effort of abstraction, which to persons who are stiffened in their prejudices, and frozen in their *selfishness*, appears utterly unreasonable: accordingly, to do to others as we would *not* that they should do unto us, is no very uncommon practical rendering of that passage.

Those who imagine that a system of parsimony is the only foundation on which to rear the prosperity of their families, are, as is the case with most errors, insuring an effect directly contrary to their aim ; for they could not devise a more effectual means of disposing them to extravagance and prodigality. There are not wanting instances in the recollection of many to prove, that where property has been needlessly hoarded, it has been as need-

lessly dissipated when it came into the hands
of children from whom it had been so withheld. It is not the nature of the human mind
to take a favourable direction under oppressive discipline of any kind; injustice exaspe-
rates it : to whatever extreme it passes, it will
be alike remote from virtue and from happiness. The worst of parents would not
willingly foster in the minds of his children
the unnatural wish for his own death; yet
how inevitably does a system of rigour and
tyranny, and meanness, tend to render the
idea of emancipation (by whatever means) at
least very supportable ! " When my father
dies, we'll set the parish bells a-ringing," said
a young man to his brother. " Not with my
money," replied the old gentleman, who
unfortunately happened to be within hearing !
And he was as good as his word. Such
filial sentiments are the reward, the *just* reward of oppression; yet the oppressor, the
hard man is frequently so unreasonable, so
ignorant of human nature, as to be surprised
that he is not beloved by his family, and to
complain of their ingratitude and deficiency
in respect and esteem !

But the errors of parents are perhaps more frequent on the opposite extreme : by indulging their families in extravagant demands, they engender evils equally great; so is wealth perverted in various ways! A moderate portion of it is in itself a *good*, if corrupt passions did not convert it into an evil. "Take away the *dross* from the silver, and there shall come forth a vessel for the refiner."

The prayer which requested neither poverty nor riches, was founded on a just estimate of human nature : and those parents who are capable of making it, will early habituate their children to a *moderation* in their desires, as well as to frugality in their expenditure. There is no rank or circumstances in life which can render a liberal economy unnecessary

CHAP. VI.

RISING RANK IN LIFE.

———

" With my staff I passed over this Jordan, and now I am become two bands.   GENESIS, xxxii. 10.

———

IT sometimes happens that a worthy couple in humble life are rewarded for years of industry and prudence, by unexpected success in their affairs: from indigence and obscurity, they rise perhaps to comfort and affluence: but as no temporal good exists without alloy, they feel (if they are people of sense) that the want of cultivation and good-breeding, from which their former habits of life debarred them, prevents their sustaining that place in society which they might otherwise have taken, but to which money alone cannot entitle any one.   With laudable ambition they resolve that their children shall not labour under similar disadvantages; they bestow on them what is commonly termed an *education,*

and expect in due time to be amply rewarded
for the cost and solicitude in their general improvement—especially by a return of grateful
affection. The governess and masters having
performed their part, deliver up their accomplished charge; who return home to delight
their admiring parents, and astonish surrounding friends.

And now with their children's assistance
they rapidly climb the eminence which had
hitherto appeared inaccessible: of the blessings of society they enjoy as much, and perhaps more, than their hearts could wish;
but of the imperfection attending all sublu-
nary things they have another impressive lesson; for while they now find themselves recognised abroad, they are scarcely noticed at
home: here they are viewed, rather as incum-
brances, than as promoters of the general
happiness. Their inveterate habits and prejudices exercise all the patience and skill of
their more enlightened children, who some-
times-give up the case as hopeless, and content themselves with keeping their rustic
parents as much as possible in the back-
ground, treating them at best with that shy-

ness and indifference due to interlopers, and troublesome impediments to the completion of their high-flown schemes.

If this description be not totally imaginary, if the circumstances and conduct of any young readers should answer to it, a moment's reflection might convince them that these things ought not to be so. To whom are such children indebted for the advantages on which they so highly value themselves, but to those very parents whom they might have resembled in all their rude habits and vulgar prejudices, but for their superintending care? Such persons have never experienced (and it is hoped their subsequent conduct may never oblige them to experience) the anxieties, hardships, and toil, to which their parents were exposed in early life. Every comfort their children enjoy may have been purchased by a privation; every luxury by a laborious effort; every hour of cheerfulness and hilarity in the society of their equally thoughtless companions, by days of unremitting toil and restless nights of care. And are they thus rewarded?—Are the equipments with which they have so liberally furnished their

children for their entrance into life, to be
converted into hostile instruments, and
plunged as poniards into those hearts, round
every fibre of which their children's happiness has been entwined? Unfortunately for
such characters, that book which says, " De-
spise not thy mother when she is old," has
made no exception for cases of this nature :
the command is positive and unqualified,
whatever disproportion may exist between
the mental faculties or attainments of parents
and children.

It is the error of vulgar minds to entertain
false notions respecting *gentility*. In families like these there is frequently a radical
mistake on the subject. It is a quality which,
if genuine, must have its foundation in principle and moral rectitude. The skilful ana-
lizer of character may sometimes discern the
principle in uneducated parents, while not
a particle of it appears to exist in their
more accomplished children. There may be
true superiority of *character,* where there is
none of *manner;* therefore, before children
harbour sentiments or adopt conduct to the
disadvantage of their parents in this respect,

they should be well assured, from a general acquaintance with human nature, and an accurate knowledge of their individual characters, that they are as destitute of one as of the other.

Parents, however, who are conscious of a deficiency in their manners arising from such causes, should endeavour, for the general credit and respectability of their families, to conform themselves to their rising circumstances; till they have in some degree effected this, their work is incomplete. Their residence and their accommodations of every kind being on a higher scale,—having thrown off the humble garb of former days to wear the mantle of affluence, it is desirable that their carriage and conduct should harmonize as far as possible with these external appendages. This will be thought difficult— and so indeed it is; for it is not so easy a thing to lay aside a vulgar habit, as to throw off a shabby cloke: but although no exertions in after-life can supply the place of a liberal education, and although much refinement of mind and manner cannot be expected, yet it is not a hopeless task to aim at some

exterior improvement, nor to endeavour to
acquire some enlargement of views, and libe-
rality of sentiment. Those who have achieved
so much by their own strenuous exertions, have
surely not so exhausted their energies, as to be
incapable of making an additional effort to
render the whole complete. If such persons
cannot *themselves* see beyond the surface, let
them be assured there are those who *can,*
whose penetrating eye will quickly discern
vulgarity stampt in legible characters. if not
on all they *have,* at least on all they *do* and
say. Children are certainly to be commiser-
ated, whose parents will obstinately persist in
exposing their families to ridicule by habits
and manners, which a little trouble and attention might, in some degree at least, polish
and refine.

Persons who have been accustomed to
menial occupations in early life, and to the low
manners and contracted notions which these
are apt to produce, are more likely to be confirmed in them, than to rise above them as
old age advances, without strenuous resolu-
tions and endeavours to the contrary. When
other advantages are on the wane, it is espe-

cially desirable for persons in every station,
not only to cultivate an intrinsic respectability
of character, but also that pleasingness of manner which should result from it, and which is
no despicable substitute for the fascinations
of youth, or the substantial powers of mature
age.

Let us reverse the subject.—" The race
is not invariably to the swift nor the
battle to the strong." Neither the advantages of fortune, nor the most vigilant
efforts of human care and industry, can ward
off the stroke of adversity, when inflicted by
Him who has all events at His disposal.
" Except the Lord build the house, they labour in vain who build it. Except the Lord
keep the city, the watchman waketh but in
vain."—It happens not unfrequently, that
after parents have past the prime of their days
in circumstances of affluence, lavishing on
their families all those indulgences to which
their fond hearts have prompted them, that
they experience a sad reverse in their declining
years, and are reduced to a state of indigence
or dependance. Should the circumstances of
their children be more prosperous, *now* is the

season to put the genuineness of their affection, as well as the rectitude of their principles to the proof. There was a time when
the helpless state of infancy called forth all
the tender exertions of those who were bound
by nature to cherish and protect it; the circumstances of the parties are now reversed,
but the obligation remains unchanged. Can
it be necessary to make an appeal to the justice or to the gratitude of any individual,
whose most attached, disinterested, and persevering friend—in one comprehensive word,
whose *parent*—now in turn claims succour and
protection? Must we *plead* for such a one?
Many have been reduced to circumstances of
dependance on their children, by having with
a short-sighted fondness gratified their every
wish in former times, and yielded to all their
unreasonable demands. But is it for these
children to inflict the punishment? Should
they repay their parents' past indulgence with
present ingratitude?—Parents whose earthly
wishes were bounded by the future prosperity
of their families, although they were unhappily
deficient in the most effectual means of secur-
ing it. Is *this* the time to rouse them from

their pleasing dreams? And shall the objects
of their fondest attachment undertake the
task? When the infirmities of nature begin to
assail them; when surrounding objects which
were heretofore accustomed to delight, lose their
fascinations; when every step they advance
towards the confines of these mortal shores
becomes more rugged and difficult; it ill suf-
fices to be presented with a staff to pursue the
remaining journey—with something just to
prevent the tottering frame from sinking.—
Nature now requires the gentle arm to support, the soothing voice of kindness to cheer,
the warm mantle of filial love to protect from
the chilling blast: but a bare sustenance dispensed as a charitable boon to a stranger,
rather than as the voluntary offering of filial
and well-earned affection, is hard fare indeed.

Are there any who anticipate the time
with secret complacency, when they shall be
relieved even from such services as these?—
Well, be not impatient, time is doing his
office: he keeps a steady pace with your parents, and with yourselves too—the weeks,
and months, and years, are taking their flight
as rapidly, one would think, as a mortal could

wish. Soon, very soon, although it may seem long to you,—that tottering frame which now bears so heavily on you, will need no further support, but will crumble into dust, and " the worm shall feed sweetly on it." And can you anticipate this with satisfaction ?—The time was, when if your infant frame had thus sunk even before you had rendered one service, or afforded any reward but your smiles, that the hearts of your parents would have been torn with the keenest anguish. You were conducted by them through all the common perils of your infancy and childhood with anxious solicitude, and the most assiduous care ; they congratulated themselves to see their labours crowned with success, at whatever expense. Now they have thus far completed their task, and brought you to maturity. " Rejoice, O young man, in thy youth, and walk in the sight of thine eyes," although the desire of their eyes should extort many a briny tear from them ; " but know, that for all these things God shall bring thee into judgment!"

If those who harden their hearts against

the poor and the needy, and turn away their
eyes from the fatherless and the *stranger*, in-
cur the divine displeasure, in how much
greater degree do they offend, who, regardless of nature's ties, and of the strongest of
all human obligations, withhold from a ne-
cessitous parent what it is in their power to
afford, whether in the way of sustenance, or
in those tender offices which are equally ac-
ceptable, and far more endearing, and which
all, whether rich or poor, imperiously need
under the infirmities of age, or the decays of
nature! Or, if they are dealt out with a nig-
gardly hand, mistaking that for duty done,
which is destitute of its most essential quality—*filial affection!*

The possibility of such a requital should
operate as an additional motive with parents
to instil sterling principles into their children;
and by every possible means to cherish that
tenderness of heart, that general benevolence,
which embraces all within its sphere, and
each according to its specific claim; then,
and then only, are parents secure. But should
Providence see fit to render them dependant
on their offspring, however imperious are

their claims, they certainly should be careful
not to urge them too rigidly, especially when
their children have rising families of their
own, and their pecuniary resources are circumscribed : in that case, the weight of a parent's support, however cheerfully borne, may
become exceedingly oppressive, and the truly
considerate will bear no heavier than circumstances absolutely require. There have been
parents who, because it best suited their own
immediate interests, have held their children
in celibacy, and selfishly prevented them from
forming connexions which might have proved the happiness of their lives. It would be
much more to their credit, and perhaps to
their real advantage, to let things take their
natural course, and trust Providence with the
issue. Those who do evil that good may
come, must eventually be disappointed.

CHAPTER VII.

PARENTAL AND FILIAL CONDUCT, AS IT RELATES TO
THE SEXES.

_____

" That our sons may be as plants grown up in their
youth; that our daughters may be as corner stones, polish-
ed after the similitude of a palace."

PSALM cxliv. 12.

_____

FILIAL duties, generally speaking, are of universal application; but there are some, which
as they relate exclusively to sex, may be
worthy of distinct consideration.

The sons in most families are transferred
from the nursery to the school, and from
thence to the practice of some business or
profession, and can have comparatively but
little intercourse with their mothers; it is,
therefore, to those who remain stationary beneath the paternal roof that the following

hints are chiefly applicable; they may, however, be found sufficiently general to affect, in
some degree, the conduct of sons whether at
home or abroad.

It is no equivocal symptom of amiableness
of disposition, when two individuals, totally
opposite in their occupations, habits, and pursuits, dwell together in unity : when a mother and her sons do so, it redounds greatly to
the credit of both : but this is not universally
the case, even where there is no deficiency of
natural affection, no unkind intention on
either side.   The evil frequently originates in
that thoughtlessness, which seems to be a
marked characteristic of the male sex in early
life. With some gentlemen indeed it is requisite, that a lady should be *young*, to entitle
her to any consideration ; although to witness
their manner to a *female*, an *aged female*, and
that female their *mother*, excites a doubt of their
entertaining any genuine respect for the sex.
Certainly she is in no very enviable situation,
whose lot it is to dwell under the roof with
such high-flown spirits. They deem her pursuits trivial and unimportant; although to
such, perhaps, they are indebted for life and

health, and for many of the comforts they
now enjoy, but know not how to appreciate.
Is it then a trivial pursuit to rear a family?—
to bring up valuable members of society,
such as, probably, they deem themselves to
be! Their very self-importance might raise
her in their esteem, as being the instrument,
although an humble one, of so much good to
the world. Let every young woman, however, beware of him who manifests such sentiments by his conduct; for he who is remiss
in one relation, will generally prove so in
another. Where good principle exists, its influence is not partial. The most satisfactory
pledge for her own happiness that a young
woman can desire, is the respectful conduct of
a son to his mother. Such as he is under the
parental roof, such in all probability he will
prove under his own. His dignity as a man, as
well as a Christian, is not impaired but enhanced
by the minutest attentions to an aged parent.
King Solomon in all his glory never appeared
to greater advantage than in the polite reception he gave to his mother, when she appeared
before him with the request of Adonijah.
But to the honour of the sex, and of human

nature, we have no occasion to recur to the
records of antiquity for bright examples of
filial duty; such instances, we hope, are familiar to the majority of our readers. It is true,
as they pass under their observation they will
be appreciated by them according to their
own particular sentiments and dispositions.
There are some, perhaps, who would have
scoffed at the conduct of two young men of
sense and intelligence, whose aged mother
was busily employed in executing a piece of
needle-work equally void of taste and utility.
So far from ridiculing or slighting her performance, as it beguiled the tedious hours of
an infirm parent, they appeared to take a
lively interest in it; and thereby afforded an
instance of that endearing *sympathy*, which
is so universally requisite in all our intercourse with others, but which is yet so spar-
ingly exercised, although one of the sweetest
ingredients in the cup of domestic life. Such
characters stand well opposed to those whose
prevailing system is *tormenting*; who from
commencing their operations with their
mothers, proceed with their experiments on
their sisters, their younger brothers, the

servants, and of course all the unfortunate animals within doors and without, who may chance to come in their way. In such feats there may certainly be much *wit*, and *prowess*, and *spirit*; but manly feeling, and true dignity, and proper spirit, display themselves very differently; and, on every account, the sooner they are acquired the better.

It were to be wished that some sons, for their own sakes, would pay a little more respect to their mother's feelings, in what relates to their general health; that they would not altogether reject her services, either in preserving or recovering it. This is a matron's appropriate province: in all common cases, a prudent mother may safely be confided in, (for a *prudent* mother will not interfere with what is beyond her reach). A sensible woman, independently of the general advantages of experience, of observation, and perhaps of reading, must be furnished with additional skill in the management of her own family, from her more intimate knowledge of their constitutions. Some who have not been sufficiently aware of this, have paid dearly for their incredulity.

But an address to *daughters*, in reference
to their mothers, appears still more appropriate from the intimate and frequently pro-
tracted connexion which subsists between
them. *They* especially should be solicitous
to discharge the duties of that relation in
which others may one day stand to themselves; and although the inequality of years
must certainly produce some essential differ-
ence in their feelings and pursuits, yet there
are points in which they as naturally correspond.

The happiness of a mother is *essentially*
at the mercy of the female branches of her
family; and her condition is to be commise-
rated, if in the prospect of succeeding years
spent under the same roof with them, when
her health and spirits are on the wane, they
manifest no inclination to promote her comfort. *External* attentions will not suffice to
discharge the duties of this intimate relation.
The services of one who is not her mother's
confidential friend, are of little comparative
value; while that bosom which is the receptacle of every maternal care and sorrow,
thereby becomes the repository of such a

knowledge of the world, as may be of essential service when her own turn comes to encounter it.

It is truly revolting to a feeling mind, to behold a *mother* and a *daughter*—those dear relations—if not actually at variance, evidently not on terms of intimacy and confidence. If the former be respectable and affectionate, it is a phenomenon for which it is difficult to account, except from some radical error in the education.

A judicious mother will adapt her conduct, as well to the sexes, as to the dispositions of her children. Those who do not receive the same degree of attention from their sons as from their daughters, should make every allowance which the nature of things admits, and should not be too hasty in attributing to want of affection what may be the mere effect of thoughtlessness, united with different pursuits and avocations.

She who through an excess of maternal anxiety would shield her son from every wind that blows, is placing herself in the predicament of a hen with a duckling brood, who will follow the dictates of their nature, and sail away, rejecting her care, and regardless of her call. To those who might submit to it, such superabundant care would prove highly injurious both to body and mind, and must expose them to the ridicule of their associates. One of the most essential services which a mother can render to her resident sons, is by every prudent means to instil into them a taste and relish for domestic life. The rational and satisfactory pleasures of a cheerful and happy home, will render them more cautious than they might otherwise be in the choice of their connexions,—better aware of what qualities are most requisite in fire-side companions, as well as more affectionate in their subsequent conduct towards them. Let their esteem for the sex be founded on the character of their *mother*, than which nothing can more effectually contribute to their individual respectability.

That familiar aphorism of Scripture, that " those who would have friends must shew themselves friendly," is in no instance more forcibly exemplified than in the intercourse between parents and children. She who would find a confidential friend in her

daughter, must previously set the example.
Let that solace and security which during infancy she experienced in the maternal bosom,
increase with her years. A morose and distant carriage is as inimical to filial confidence,
as a trifling levity of manner, which forfeits
all title to it. Where it does exist (as was
before hinted,) it affords special opportunities
for general instruction, and for conveying
useful knowledge. Every new circumstance
supplies matter for judicious observation,
warning, or counsel. It is not so much by
prosing lessons that young persons are essentially benefitted, as by appropriate hints resulting from the occasion, and skilfully applied
according to the disposition and circumstances
of the pupil; but it is obvious that the most
entire cordiality is necessary to give opportu-
nity for, or poignant effect to, such lessons.

It cannot be too frequently repeated, that
one essential part of domestic education con-
sists in rendering home agreeable; not, indeed,
by those frivolities which the ignorant select
for that purpose, but by those rational pleasures which are calculated to expand the
mind, and give a right bias to the taste and

feelings : even the remote effects of this are
incalculable.   To adopt the sentiments of a
recent publication.* "Let each individual have
to look back with tender remembrance on
the hours, the places, and the associates, where
the world first dawned on his mental energies. In the journey of life he seems to draw
a lengthened chain, from this innocent, this
lovely region, to which the aged mind ever
reverts with pleasure and complacency. The
recollection of the playful sports of childhood
solaces the imagination and the memory, in
the evening of life, as if man, like a plant,
were physically attached to the spot on which
he blossomed."

Domestic felicity in early life restrains the
passion for dissipation, and may prevent the
forming improper connexions, which sometimes originate in the mere desire of quitting
the paternal roof, and seeking that happiness
from foreign sources which is not to be found
at home. Early comfort diffuses an air of
pleasing serenity over the whole deportment,
and frequently renders the happy subject of it

* Boyne on the Human Species.

proof against that *irritableness,* which the
subsequent cares and sorrows of life are apt to
engender.

The daughter who loves her home will
take a lively interest in all its concerns, and be
solicitous to promote the happiness of the
little circle of which she forms a part; especially if her mother is able and willing to
instruct and assist her. If she be desirous
that her daughter should rank with herself
in domestic qualifications, she will not,
either by a false tenderness, or a criminal negligence, suffer her to remain ignorant of such
things as her future station in life may
require her to be acquainted with: this would
not only render her helpless and ridiculous,
in a situation the most responsible, but would
be treating with the greatest ingratitude the
man who lays his fortune and his future happiness and respectability at her daughter's feet.
There are not wanting those, who have
groaned under the effects of such maternal
negligence for many years of married life.

Next in importance to religious instruction, is that general knowledge, that mental
cultivation, which is to be obtained (and only

to be obtained) by habits of *reading,* and
which must assuredly rank amongst the most
indispensable qualifications of a female ; not
only to render her a suitable companion for
an intelligent partner, but as it is eminently
calculated to enable her to fulfil every duty
of her station. We are aware that this assertion would surprise many mothers among
the middling classes, who being destitute of
these advantages themselves, ignorantly conclude that such pursuits must be inimical to
domestic proficiency. It is granted, that in common with any other desirable object, they may
be suffered to engross an undue share of time
and attention : but the possibility of abusing a
thing is no argument against it ; and we are
well persuaded that there is far less danger
of this being the case with regard to mental
improvement, than with some other things
at which these same persons are not always
so ready to take the alarm ; frivolities,
(which, if not encouraged in their daughters,
are but too seldom *discouraged* by the mothers to whom we allude) are far more frequently found to interfere with, and to give
a distaste to, the more important domestic

F

concerns, than a love of reading. So far from
estranging a woman from the discharge of
her appropriate duties, the direct tendency of
knowledge, and of that enlarged view of
things which it affords, is to shew her what
they are, to convince her of their propriety
and importance, and to qualify her to fulfil
them in a rational and systematic manner :
hence it is that the *kitchen,* no less than the
parlour and the *nursery,* partake the happy
effects of the superintendance of an *intelligent*
mistress.

It is true that instances might be produced
of women, who, although they have not enjoyed the advantages of mental cultivation,
are yet seen to perform the duties of their
station with singular propriety and address,
and to whom the honourable titles of *good*
wives and mothers justly belong; for good
sense, united with sound principle, will go
far towards qualifying a person for any station. In such cases, the intelligent observer
is ready to exclaim, " What women would
these have been, with minds well stored and
cultivated by reading !" But notwithstanding
these instances, a very slight observation is

sufficient to show, that the majority of uninformed women suffer greatly in themselves
and in their families from the deficiency.
Their houses, indeed, may be neat and orderly; their dinners may be well served; and
such mothers may so far possess the gift of
management, as to scold, or bribe, or drill
their progeny into something like order and
obedience; but we must not expect to see
these persons act upon system, nor can the
permanent effects of a rational system follow;
that system, which especially makes it the
grand interest, and happiness, and amusement,
of the intelligent mother to educate her children. She leaves her pleasures when she
leaves her home, and returns to it as from a
banishment.

The duties, of whatever description, which
emanate from a mind enlightened and ex-
panded by knowledge, will maintain an evident superiority over such as result from
mere habit, or even from an uninformed
sense of duty; for a narrow mode of thinking
and acting is the inseparable companion of
ignorance. Will she who has acquired some
general knowledge of the world in which she

lives, conduct the affairs of her own province
with less skill than she whose ideas are circumscribed to the narrow spot on which she
vegetates, incapable of extending them beyond the visible objects around her? Will not
she who has taken even a transient survey of
men and things in distant ages and countries,
be better qualified to encounter her own personal emergencies and vicissitudes, than she
who has no other guide to direct her than the
impulse of the moment, or the customs and
notions prevalent among her neighbours, who
are probably no better informed than herself?
The contemplation of virtue and of vice, of
wisdom and of folly, as exhibited in characters public or private, which history and bio-
graphy display, stimulate to worthy actions;
while a moderate acquaintance with works of
taste, would prove of what human intellect
is capable, and awaken a salutary admiration of things that are truly excellent, instead
of its being wasted on the trifles that amuse
vulgar minds.

A cultivated taste, independant of present
gratification, is one of the most valuable of
human resources under the trials and daily

vexations of life: it is even a useful hand-maid to religion, although some narrow-minded people may feel offended at the asser-tion.—Offended, because they never availed themselves of her services. Especially is it an antidote against that insipidity of charac-ter—that trifling insignificance, which tends to bring our sex into disesteem and contempt; which incapacitates them from sustaining a part in rational or instructive conversation, and which renders old age worse than unin-teresting.

Would those who have the superintend-ance of youth, endeavour to give them a just estimate of the *advantages* resulting from those things they attempt to teach, instead of enforcing them as tasks, their labours would more frequently be crowned with success, and the most scrupulous mother might banish all apprehensions as to the *domestic habits* of a daughter so instructed. If a young woman has once been rendered domestic upon *prin-ciple*, there is little reason to fear, that when pursuits of a more elevated nature solicit a portion of her attention, they should destroy those habits which are so congenial to the

female character, and which form, as it were,
a part of her nature. The mind that is trained to an accurate estimate of the importance
of objects, will duly apportion the time requisite to the pursuit of each. This is a most
essential lesson in education, and should be
sedulously instilled by parental *example* as
well as by precept. It should enforce this
important truth, that even duty is no longer
such than while it occupies its appropriate
time and place. The moment that one duty
encroaches on another, it degenerates into a
fault.

Let mothers then, we repeat, who are so
jealous of the time which is devoted to objects which themselves are not qualified to
appreciate, take especial care that it be not
squandered on pursuits still more inimical to
domestic proficiency; on that species of expensive show and dissipation by which it is
so often suffered to glide away, producing
effects directly contrary to individual or social
advantage. Were a sense of the high importance and value of time carefully impressed
upon the young mind in early life, neither
reading, nor any less worthy pursuit, would

be suffered to encroach upon other useful and necessary occupations.

Let it be remembered, that it will not suffice to qualify daughters exclusively for wedlock. It is the lot, or the choice, of some to remain single; and a judicious mother will endeavour to prepare them also for a life of celibacy, and to furnish them with resources for solitary hours. She will not accustom them to think the marriage state essential to happiness, or that alone for which all their acquirements are intended to prepare them. They are sometimes called to services of a different nature, and it is honourable that these should be cheerfully and zealously performed. The all wise Disposer has something for every one to do, the single as well as the married; and in times like the present, when individual activity is so much required, persons who are unencumbered by domestic concerns, are especially called upon to go and work in God's vineyard; nor are they in numberless honourable instances called upon in vain. There never was a period since the apostolic days when that assertion was more strikingly exemplified, " that she who is unmarried

careth for the things of the Lord, how she
may serve the Lord." Let it then be the endeavour of parents to make their daughters
good women; and thus, whether married or
single, they will prove ornaments and blessings to society.

CHAPTER VIII.

PARTIALITY.

"Bless me, even me also, O my Father!"

GENESIS, xxvii. 34.

THAT children of the same family, who
stand in an equal relation, should not equally
share in the affections of their parents, is a
lamentable instance of the perversity of
human nature. When these prejudices are
entertained during infancy, before the subjects of them can have done either good or
harm, they must be the effect of caprice, and
are a species of injustice which admits of no
defence. Our Creator, our fellow-creatures,
and the lower orders of creation, unite to condemn it. Well will it be if those who indulge it should ultimately join in the general
censure, and with sentiments of that deep

contrition which would well become them,
return to their proper feelings, and restore their
injured offspring to their natural rights.

That child is in a worse than orphan condition who, dwelling under the parental roof,
has not a due share in a parent's affection .
especially if, during infancy and childhood,
when nature points it to its natural guardians
and protectors, it is repelled by coldness or
unkindness ; it is but too probable, that when
the best and earliest affections of the heart
are thus turned out of their proper channel,
they may take a wrong direction, and become
the source of much misery to their connec-
tions. Those who feel the slightest inclination thus to pervert the laws of nature, would
be wise in resisting it in its early stages, and
expelling the impulse from their bosoms, as
they would the most noxious reptile which
should attempt to harbour there. Such a
prejudice is replete with all the evils with
which a family can be visited. Jealousy,
hatred, discord, with the calamities naturally
engendered by them, are in its train. The
consequences are frequently as injurious to
the rest of the family, as to the unhappy ob-

ject against whom the prejudice exists. Fra-
ternal affection is one of the earliest lessons
to be instilled into the young mind by the
natural guardians of family peace ; but if they
arm brother against brother by their own
unjust and partial conduct, who can answer
for the consequences ?

But this is a case which less frequently
occurs, and, however, gloomy its aspect, is
less injurious in its effects than the opposite
error of *favouritism*. Woe to the child who
is detached from the rest of his family by the
distinguishing affection of his parents! It
requires more disinterestedness and self-com-
mand than falls to the lot of human nature in
general, and of youth in particular, to sustain a rectitude and amiableness of character
under circumstances so trying to both. Ill
judging parents, while thus distinguishing
the objects of their supreme affection, are,
probably, in the same proportion, accumulating for them more disappointments and
sorrows than might otherwise fall to their
share : the consequences of excess of indulgence, and of that idea of self-importance
which the *favourite* naturally conceives. The

world into which they are preparing to enter
will not be partial; they will be no favourites
there beyond their just deserts. Society is
now waiting, with all its various instruments
of discipline, to effect that which ought to
have been accomplished under the paternal
roof: well will it be for the pupil if this discipline at last prove salutary.

It is acknowledged that families often
manifest a great inequality in the natural
amiableness of their tempers, and the pleasingness of their manners. But although the
character of some children cannot be contem-
plated with the same delight as that of others,
their persons should be regarded with equal
affection; the love of benevolence may be
powerful, where the love of complacency is
but faint: when this is the case, the extra
discipline required will be carefully and judiciously administered; the result, not of passion, but of principle. When the chastised
party can discover no injustice or partiality
in what is inflicted, it is much more likely to
prove salutary; an opposite conduct would
only aggravate the evil, and render the object
of unnecessary severity still more untoward.

To children who are placed in either of
the above perilous situations, a word of advice
may not be unseasonable. Let the few who
come under the former description continue
in patient well-doing, notwithstanding all
discouragements. There have been those,
who in similar circumstances, by persevering assiduities and attentions to their
parents, have entirely overcome their unnatural prejudices, and have completely reinstated
themselves in their fond affections. Nor let
them forget, that no misconduct of their parents can absolve them from their own personal obligations: as was before observed,
the fifth commandment is of universal application—it has no exceptions. In their steady
obedience they have this promise for their
support, that "when their father and their mother forsake them, then the Lord will take
them up." They have an Almighty parent,
who is especially the guardian and protector
of the destitute and oppressed. He is no re-
specter of persons; His mercy and His justice
are equally engaged to plead their cause, and
to defend their rights. He has all hearts in
His hands, and is able to turn the affections of

their parents towards them, or to give them
favour in the sight of others, who may amply
supply their place.   Common policy, indeed,
would suggest that they should afford no reasonable pretence for disapprobation.

This, however, with all its disadvantages,
let it be repeated, is a situation far less perilous than that of one who has the *misfortune*
to be a favourite   Let those, however, who
are thus distinguished, be especially solicitous
to deserve it. When perehed on the eminence,
where by their parents' unjust partiality they
are placed, let them not treat their brethren
beneath with scorn or neglect, especially should
their filial duty and affection keep pace with
their distinguished privileges. It should never
be said that those who enjoy the greatest
share of their parents' love, manifest the least
towards them in return.   It, however, frequently happens, that children thus circumstanced become the instruments of deserved
punishment to those very parents; and when
the purpose is accomplished, they are broken in
pieces, and thrown aside as things vile and
hurtful, by a retributive Providence.

It is much to the credit of those who re-

main proof against the injurious influence of
such circumstances.   Prosperity is always
dangerous, but especially so during the season
of youth, and that species of it which is calculated to engender conceit and self-importance is of the most baneful kind. Yet a situation thus unfavourable, may afford important
lessons on some future day.   The result may
eventually place the fallacy of human schemes
and expectations in a striking point of view.
Time may shew that what was designed by
unjust partiality for the interest of a favourite,
has become a snare and a trap, and that less
indulgence, however uncongenial to present
feeling, would on the whole have been more
advantageous.   Such children may live to see
those of their brethren who were not so distinguished by parental affection, and over
whom perhaps they had been suffered to rule
and tyrannize, get the start of them in life; and
the lot of each may be cast by an over-ruling
power into a situation directly the reverse
of paternal plans. Possibly the unjust course
pursued, may be the very means of producing
such contrary effects. The fallible children of
men are disposed to call good evil, and evil

good; they pursue the one and avoid the other, in direct opposition to their own real interests. But He whose thoughts are not as our thoughts, nor His ways as our ways, often sees fit to frustrate our schemes, and make our own perverse passions instrumental to the fulfilment of his purposes. Happy are we, if after all His fatherly discipline, we discern His hand;—yea, happy are we, if we wisely observe these things : then shall we not fail to see the loving kindness of the Lord, in the midst of our bitterest disappointments.

Such sentiments (if they needed it) might find ample confirmation in the history of Jacob, who was driven from his paternal home, and became an exile in a distant land, through the partiality of his mother. There he suffered under the effects of that deceit which he had himself been taught to practise, and which, on his return, endangered the lives of his family, though perpetrated years before they were born. But the reward of such conduct has been witnessed in many a sorrowful instance since his day, and will yet be witnessed wherever it is adopted.

CHAP. IX.

SETTLING IN LIFE.

———

"But happy they, the happiest of their kind,
Whom gentler stars unite, and in one fate
Their hearts, their fortunes, and their beings blend."
                                        THOMSON.

———

WHETHER parents have themselves been happy in the married state or not, they are equally qualified to appreciate the importance of the connexion; knowing, as they must, upon what it is that conjugal felicity depends, one should not expect them to sacrifice the happiness of their children to caprice, to fortune, or to ambition; or, last of all, to their own interests: yet that this has been done too frequently, must be in the painful recollection of many. Whether one human being (although a parent) has the future happiness of another at

such absolute disposal, is a question which
neither reason nor justice would find it difficult to decide.   Coercive measures, however,
are more justifiable (especially towards a
young lady in her teens) in *preventing* a connexion, than in forming one.   The former
measure may be only the suspension of happiness, the latter may prove its final termination.   " Till death us do part," is a sentence
which should deeply impress, and be carefully
deposited in the memory of every married
couple, against the time when their children
may claim assistance and advice in a matter
of such vast, such vital importance.   How
can a parent endure to hear such an irrevocable vow, forced from the lips of one of whose
happiness, every natural tie, every moral
and religious principle has made him the
guardian!   Especially, how can *she* who has
spent so many happy years with the partner
of her choice, the object of her tenderest affections,—how can she resign her child to one
from whom her heart revolts?   Or how can
a mother who has been a stranger to connubial happiness, who has dragged on so many
tedious years in irksome bondage, force her

daughter into the same dreary thraldom?—
Is it that the charms of gold, with the pleasures or the consequence it may have purchased
for her, have so occupied every avenue of her
soul as to have left no aching void—as to have
proved successful substitutes for connubial
felicity?—If so, her notions of genuine happiness are not very correct—not such as
should place that of another at her disposal.

The following circumstance, well known
to the writer, may serve to illustrate the criminality, as well as the impolicy, of forced
marriages. A young lady, with the approbation of her family, had permitted her affections
to be engaged by a gentleman, with whom
there appeared every reason to anticipate a
propitious union: when, however, he imagined himself sure of her, he manifested a
peevishness of temper, and propensity to covetousness, which many take greater pains to
conceal until they have secured their object.
For a long time, however, her attachment remained unshaken, till at length it gave way
under repeated provocations: she ceased to
love one whom she could no longer esteem,
and the union was given up by mutual con-

sent. In process of time she was again addressed by a gentleman, apparently more deserving: and the connexion promised the
happiest results, till their felicity was interrupted by the intemperate conduct of her
former lover, whose attachment was again
revived from this circumstance, and which
manifested itself by threatening destruction to
his rival, to the object of his affections, and
to himself.   As he was connected in business
with the young lady's father, he could not
disengage himself without considerable incon-
venience to the family.   Under these circumstances, they resolved to sacrifice her happiness to their own interest;   and while the
father imprecated vengeance on her head,
should she persevere in her refusal, the mother, better skilled in the arts of persuasion,
besought her consent to the union on her
knees!—Thus beset on every side, and with
a heart torn by contending passions, she
relinquished the object of her sincerest attachment, and yielded her hand to the man who,
but for his own misconduct, would never have
known a rival.   She had the grief to see her
discarded friend expire in a few months in a

state of mental derangement, the consequence of his severe disappointment.

The subsequent conduct of her husband but too well justified her apprehensions, and put her truly meek and patient temper to the severest trial. The depressing effects on her mind were such as might have been expected; although naturally formed for domestic life, she never *shone* either as a wife or mother. Her family evidently suffered no less than herself from the consequences of this early oppression.

The deep contrition evinced by her husband in her dying moments, could neither protract her existence, nor recal his past misconduct;—the performance of duty to *living* relatives, is of much more value than the most humiliating concessions to *dying* ones.

Whether any advantages to be derived from a forced union can sufficiently compensate for the sacrifices it demands, and the evils with which it is almost always attended, those who have tried the experiment are, perhaps, the most competent to determine.

It is true, that at this eventful period a parent's task is most difficult and anxious. The utmost wisdom and prudence, united

with the sincerest affection, sometimes prove
of no avail.   An appeal to reason, by a fair
and candid representation of the probable
consequences of a step about to be taken,
may sometimes have a happy effect, especially
where the character has been previously formed by judicious management.   If this has not
been the case, it is indeed too much to expect
any great degree of pliability, or self command, in an affair in which the most powerful
principles of our nature are implicated.

It sometimes happens that, notwithstanding all the prudent endeavours of a parent,
the decisive step is taken, and the fate of the
object of solicitude is unalterably fixed, up to
the very confines of this mortal life.   When
this is the case, whatever previous disapprobation it may have excited, if the happiness
of the child (not the authority of the parent)
has been the primary object, it will still remain so.   To abandon a much-loved being
for one false step taken at an inexperienced
age, and which may prove its own punishment, is totally unlike the conduct of the
universal Parent, who, patient and long suffering, is accumulating benefits on the heads

of His children, notwithstanding all their re-iterated offences.

Especially should parents endeavour, if possible, to restrain their resentment against those who have obtruded into their families; for as the " twain are now become one flesh," the displeasure manifested against one, must eventually inflict pain upon the other, besides the hazard of creating discord, and making a breach between the parties, which it may be impossible afterwards to heal.

And now we have advanced thus far on the subject, let those mothers receive a caution who have a propensity to pry into, and interfere with the domestic concerns of their married children: of their advice and assistance (the result of mature experience) all prudent children will gladly avail themselves; but they should now be allowed to stand alone, unless, indeed, when they have imprudently entered into the state at a childish age. Let them learn to manage for themselves, nor, by an intolerable officiousness make them feel that their shackles are not yet removed. An arduous task they have undertaken, like their parents before them, (it is well if they are aware of it); but let them feel themselves *men* and *women*, and experience will probably do its work, and accomplish more than can ever be effected by a teasing and meddlesome interference. But to return from this digression.

There are other important concerns in life besides matrimonial connexions, which occasion much anxiety to the heads of families respecting the future destination of their children. Considerate parents will not place them in situations unequal to their talents, or repugnant to their tastes. Every one should be allowed the privilege of choosing that business or profession on which his future prospects depend; an opposite conduct is equally unfavourable to the character and the circumstances. For parents to *point* their children to that which is apparently the most prudent path, is their bounden duty; to force them into it, is both impolitic and cruel. It is hard that children should suffer to the very close of life (as they sometimes do) from the despotism of parents, who when sleeping in the dust cannot witness the sad effects of their own misconduct, or make reparation for the misery they have occasioned.

It is sometimes the fate of such persons to survive the objects of their tyranny. This was the case with a gentleman who had forced his only child into the navy, totally against his inclination. Some months after his departure, as the father was standing at his window, a woman solicited charity, saying, that her husband was lost at sea, by the foundering of such a ship, and that she herself had narrowly escaped the same fate. On inquiring if she knew Mr. —, and what befel him, she replied that she saw him perish! From that moment to the end of life he was in a state bordering on derangement: the whole of his time was occupied in travelling from place to place without an object, yet ever in haste. At his death a considerable portion of his property was dissipated in expensive litigation, from his alleged incompetency to execute a will; that property which would have been the undisputed inheritance of his only child, but for the criminal obstinacy of an unnatural father!

On the other hand, were young persons sufficiently impressed with the importance to future happiness of steps taken in early life, they would cease to wonder or to be angry at the interference of their parents, who having been taught by experience to consider consequences, wish to direct those who are too apt to look no further than the present moment, and who are so readily deceived by specious appearances. It is hard when their parents have just finished their anxious and laborious task, and now look for their reward in the completion of their hopes, the final well-being of their charge, to find them all dashed in a moment by some irremediable imprudence. It is the way to cast a deepening gloom over the evening of their life, to " bring their grey hairs with sorrow to the grave." When Rebecca said, " If Jacob should take a wife of the daughters of the land, what good shall my life do me?" she spake the language of many an anxious mother in every succeeding age.

There sometimes happens (for the credit of our sex it is of rare occurrence) an instance of female degradation, for which it is difficult to account. It is when a young woman of education connects herself with a person in low life! If there be conduct which could justify inexorable resentment in a parent, surely it is this, when, descending from the sphere in which Providence had placed her, she voluntarily plunges into vulgarity, and in so doing, sinks even beneath the level at which she aimed. Where symptoms of such depravity appear, the prospect is appalling: parents may succeed in averting immediate danger by bolts and bars; but nothing less than providential interference can afford a reasonable hope, that a mind so degraded will not eventually contrive the ruinous catastrophe.

Such disastrous connexions frequently originate in the culpable negligence of parents respecting their children's society. When this is suffered to be beneath their rank in life, uncongenial with their habits, or inconsistent with their principles, what but unhappy consequences can be expected? The following anecdote is of a kind not indeed very frequently met with, but every such occurrence should operate as a warning to parents, carefully to preserve their children from the society of their inferiors.

A young lady of fifteen, the daughter of a Baronet, was imprudently suffered by her mother (who devoted the chief of her time to the card-table) to be on terms of familiarity with one of the upper servants of the family, who happened to be a favourite; and she occasionally accompanied this person in her visits to a relation who resided in the neighbourhood, and who was a decent tradesman. The condescension on her part, and the homage paid to her rank on theirs, kept the parties in mutual good humour, and occasioned a frequent repetition of visits: here she became acquainted with another relation of the same family, who although he was an elderly man, by no means personable, and possessed of but little property, contrived so by his art and address to ingratiate himself with this thoughtless girl, as to prevail upon her to become his wife. At that period a trip to Gretna was not necessary, as the Savoy marriages were then valid. Having thus legally secured his prize, he by a short note communicated the unwelcome intelligence to her family: the consternation and distress into which they were thrown may be easily conceived. Her brother repaired to the house, and in a paroxysm of rage drew his sword, which he would have plunged in the bosom of his new relation, but for the interposition of the by-standers. This, however, was of no avail; the deed was done, and the inconsolable family were compelled to abandon the unfortunate victim to her fate. That a total degeneracy of character was the consequence of such a step, taken at so early an age, is not surprising. She became a widow at twenty-five; but a taste for low company, and an increasing levity of conduct, left no hopes of her ever returning to that station in society which she had voluntarily abandoned. Who can tell into what snares inexperienced youth may fall, when deserted by their natural protectors, and suffered to associate with their inferiors!

It is possible, however, to be unsuitably yoked, where there is no inequality of rank or education, or disparity of age. A variety of other circumstances might be specified, which ought to be considered as insurmountable impediments to a matrimonial union. When these are pointed out by a judicious parent, a prudent child will suffer them to have their due weight, before the affections are too warmly engaged: when, however, the alliance is formed, and the daughter, having left her father and her mother, is become one with the object of her choice, let it be remembered that those endearing ties which connect the child and the parent, cannot be disannulled by a subsequent engagement. Although she have left her parents' dwelling, the interest they manifest in the step she has taken, plainly shews that she still retains her wonted place in their affections; they should not then be expelled from hers. She has now entered on cares and interests like their own, and (if ever before) she can no longer plead dissimilarity of circumstances as an excuse for uncongenial feelings. As the head of a family, she begins to have feelings in common with them; while every day's experience will teach her to account for many things which might once be deemed strange, or even reprehensible in their conduct. And having given them a new relation, let it especially be her endeavour to promote in her partner a filial affection for their persons, and respect for their characters. It is greatly to the credit, and much to the comfort, of all parties, when a mutual good will exists between parents and their newly acquired sons and daughters.

It is but just to observe, that unsuitable matches are not exclusively confined to *young* people. Parents themselves sometimes forget what is due to their own characters, to the peace and welfare of their families, and shall we say to the memory of their deceased partners, in the imprudent connexions they form For such conduct they have obviously less excuse than their inexperienced children. In a great majority of instances, it may be fairly asserted that reason and prudence would " forbid the banns." If there is a family on either side, and especially if on both, the chances for an increase of happiness are greatly against them; particularly if the most vigilant attention has not been paid to the character of the person who is intreduecd to such an important relation. The age should unquestionably be such as to give respectability to the union. To require that daughters should yield respectful obedience to a mother scarcely older than themselves, is expecting too much from human nature. Although no decided criminality can attach to such a step, simply considered as giving grown-up children a young step-mother, yet it generally creates in by-standers a feeling which we should reluctantly indulge towards an esteemed friend: conduct which borders on the ridiculous, is destructive first of respect, and then of affection. A young lady thus introduced into a family, commonly brings (and perhaps innocently) a thousand evils in her train; nor must her doating and venerable partner be surprized if his children do not grant her that cordial reception, which, as the head of a family, he might deem her entitled to.

It would be doing violence to the feelings of the judicious reader, even to suppose the case of a widowed *mother* acting such a part! A *matron* uniting herself with a fit companion for her sons, is an action by which she forfeits every claim to the respect of society.

It is granted that cases may arise, where it shall not only be excuseable but *right* to enter a second time into the marriage state; and there is certainly no direct prohibition, either human or divine, to prevent it: yet is there not something which involuntarily commands our respect in the conduct of those

widows, who are " widows indeed?"—Who
find in the education of their children, or in
those works and labours of love, to which
their disengaged circumstances particularly
invite them, a sufficient object and interest
for the remaining years of their pilgrimage?
—But with this we have nothing to do, except as connected with the duties of parents
and children.   Let widows and widowers
marry again and again, as often as they please,
provided they do not involve their children,
who have certainly a prior claim on their affections, in the too often unhappy consequences of such connexions.   Let them, at
least, before they once more cast the die for
their own future happiness, take such precau-
tions as shall secure their families, if possible,
from the tyranny and oppression, the avarice
and cruelty, to which some unfortunate or-
phans have been exposed by second marriages.
As a pledge for her future conduct, when
a woman assumes such a situation, and a
grown-up daughter surrenders to her the
keys which were once her mother's, and have
since been her own, let her so receive them as
may at once inspire some degree of confidence

and affection. If she is a woman of principle,
she has nothing to do but to imagine herself
in her daughter's situation for a moment,
and her duty will appear plain before her.

But whatever may have been the motives
of such a person, she has certainly ventured
her own happiness on a very precarious foundation.—She has undertaken an unthankful
office, and even by a conduct the most exemplary, will find it difficult to escape the
suspicions of a censorious world. Remember
then, my *young* friends, that duty to your surviving parent, demands a quiet and becoming
acquiescence in the step he has taken, even
though the person he has chosen may not be
altogether such a one as you could have preferred. Commence the new relationship with
a polite and respectful carriage towards her:
and for this purpose, habituate yourselves to
contemplate the bright side of her character
(surely there will be some bright side to the
candid eye), and then by those little assiduities
and attentions which are ever endearing, aim
to excite her complacency and engage her
esteem. This may ripen into more tender
feelings, and lay the foundation for lasting

peace and happiness in the family.   Should
you, after all, fail in your endeavours, you
will have at least the approbation of your own
consciences, as well as of Him, who while
" to the froward He will shew himself froward," " to the upright will shew Himself
upright," by wisely and kindly superintending
all their affairs, however gloomy may be their
present aspect.

CHAPTER X.

RELIGION.

" For I know him, that he will command his children and his household after him, and they shall keep the way of the Lord."   GENESIS, xviii. 19.

"SEEK *first* the kingdom of God and his righteousness, and all other things shall be added to you," is both an appropriate admonition, and an encouraging promise, which may be well applied to parents who are solicitous for the prosperity of their children. The only solid foundation on which they can build a reasonable hope respecting them, is, their being brought up in "the nurture and admonition of the Lord." Yet it is to be deeply regretted that there are some christian parents, who, while they ardently desire the salvation of their children, are unskilled in the means best calculated to promote it, and by their injudicious conduct rather retard than accelerate their own pious designs. Parents who attempt to teaze and goad their children into religion, are not likely to convince them that " wisdom's ways are ways of *pleasantness*, and that *all* her paths are peace:" attachment to any principles, founded on a rational assent, can never be excited by coercion.

But the most exemplary conduct, the most judicious management, sometimes prove ineffectual.—" Paul may plant, and Apollos may water, but it is God alone who can give the increase." There are some children of many prayers, who still continue in the gall of bitterness, and strangers to the value of their souls;—whose language to God is, " depart from us, we desire not the knowledge of thy ways:" who say of the Saviour, " we will not have this man to reign over us." When it is even thus, the christian parent will persevere in the use of means, scattering the good seed at every convenient season, and patiently waiting to see it spring up. As a

parent he is generally favoured with many
opportunities, and his zeal should not be sur-
passed by the people of the world, who spare
no pains to give their children temporal advantages, and thereby prove that " they are
sometimes wiser in the means they adopt to
accomplish their purposes than the children
of light."

Let not parents imagine that they are fulfilling the whole of their duty, by inculcating
the bare form of religion, while negligent
respecting the power ; by suffering their children to grow up ignorant of the nature or
source of that renovating change of heart
which manifests itself in the life, and which
characterises the true Christian. There are
some professing families, who afford too much
reason to fear that they are radically deficient
in this. If so, notwithstanding all their pains,
their children are as sheep without a shep-
herd.

There are those too, who while they profess a general belief in Christianity, and affect to conform their conduct to its precepts,
go beyond a criminal negligence, and do all
in their power to impede the entrance of genu-

ine religion into the minds of their children!
incurring the censure of our Lord to the enemies of religion in His time, " That they
would not enter the kingdom of Heaven
themselves, and those who would enter they
hinder." They are angry when they perceive
a change at which they may have reason to
rejoice; but every tree is known by its fruits:
if persons who profess any change in their
religious views become thenceforward more
turbulent, self-willed, or unkind than formerly,
there is reason indeed to suspect the genuineness of their new principles, whatever they
may be; but if the reverse of this be the case,
if on a cool and unprejudiced survey of their
conduct it is evident that they are better children, that they are on the whole *improved*
characters (perfect we cannot expect them to
be), their parents have the greatest reason to
rejoice at the change, however it may have
been effected, and the probability is certainly
in favour of the supposition that they have
exchanged error for truth; for these are effects which the Gospel when rightly understood, and cordially received, never fails to

produce. But, parents, beware of mistaking a
firm conscientious obedience to the commands
of God, for turbulence, self-will, or unkindness towards yourselves. If your children are
compelled to appeal to you as the Apostles
did to their judges, and say, " Whether it be
right in the sight of God, to hearken unto
you rather than unto God, judge ye;" be assured that their resistance to your will in such
cases is justified, and that *you*, not they, are
accountable for their disobedience. But in
whatever light you may regard their conduct,
know assuredly that persecution *will not, cannot* attain your end. Persons can no more be
forced *out* of true religion, than they can be
forced *into* it. And upon the bare supposition
that the work is of God, do but consider with
whom you may be contending! Is it reasonable or safe to fight against Him? You may,
by bolts and bars, confine your children from
worshipping God in the way they have chosen,
as some have done, but you cannot utterly
preclude them from it. There is one whose
cheering presence is with them to support
and comfort, whose awful presence is with

you, to watch and restrain; to limit your power, and say " Hitherto shalt thou go, and no further."

Nor will persecution answer any desirable purpose to counteract the mere effects of delusion, the chimeras of a distempered fancy, or as you are so ready to conclude, the suggestions of vulgar enthusiasm. It is a means which ever did, and ever will defeat its own purpose: one should think that the experience of ages might by this time have banished it from human policy. Whatever there be without doors, O rear not the standard of persecution within; it is enough that *without* there are wars and fightings, but suffer not the demon of discord to gain access within your own walls. Let your resistance, should it in your conscience appear necessary, be such as may win and allure, for the wrath of man worketh not the righteousness of God. Deprive not your children of their natural birthright, liberty of conscience, especially while they yield you all the obedience in other things, which the honoured relation in which you stand can claim. The religion which they profess teaches them this, but further

they dare not go. In matters of faith, if they
are sincere, they appeal to higher authority.
Happy is the result (and it is no uncommon
one) when the mild, consistent, persevering
conduct of pious children in their religious
course, becomes the means of winning opposing parents; their prejudices gradually sub-
side, " while they behold their chaste conversation coupled with fear," till at length
their hearts are softened and prepared to receive the truth as it is in Jesus.

And when it has pleased Providence first
to call the children " from darkness to light,
let not parents proudly reject their assistance
in divine things. David says, " I am grown
wiser than my teachers;" and it is elsewhere
said, that " out of the mouths of babes and
sucklings, He has ordained strength." Those
in whom divine grace is implanted, of whatever age, become themselves as " babes de-
siring the sincere milk of the word, that they
may grow thereby." " In Christ Jesus, there
is neither male nor female, bond nor free,"
old or young; but the inquiring mind, whatever be the external circumstances, may " ask
the way to Zion" of any, whether parent or

child, who have already set their faces thither-
ward. Happy, thrice happy will it be for
your whole household, if the time should
come, " when there shall be no occasion to
say—know the Lord ; because you all know
Him, from the least even to the greatest."

It may be easily conceived, that to children sincerely religious, one of their greatest
anxieties must be the perilous situation to
which mistaken notions on this subject expose their friends and relations, and that for
those especially to whom they owe their
being, the most affectionate solicitude will be
awakened. Their solitary chambers witness
many a fervent petition on their behalf.
" Their heart's desire and prayer to God for
them is, that they may be saved." For them you
may have been laying up an ample portion
of this world's good—as, in your estimation,
the best inheritance. For you they covet the
pearl of great price, as that which they would
purchase with all their possessions. For the
temporal advantages with which you have
endowed them they are grateful; their religion does not teach them to undervalue these.
Yet they esteem all but dross, compared with

the happiness of being found in Christ, and through him possessing eternal life. May He who governs and controls all events according to the counsel of His own will, in due time unite your hearts with theirs to fear his name.

The case which has been under consideration is not novel or rare : persecution for conscience' sake, or a house divided against itself on the score of religion, is no unusual thing. Therefore those young persons who are blest with pious parents, such as are endued with knowledge and judgment to direct their anxious endeavours, should be exceedingly thankful for the advantages they enjoy, and anxious to improve them. Let it never be said, my young friends, not only that some of those who have been destitute of religious advantages have got the start of you, but that others who have every obstacle to encounter in their religious course, are willing to sacrifice all that the world holds dear, to obtain what you deem scarcely worth your pursuit. If some of your own age and circumstances view these subjects in a light so important, it behoves you, at least, to give them a serious

consideration : never forget, that where much
is given, much is required; and that it were
better for you to have been destitute of religious advantages, than that you should have
abused them. This your parents know, and
all their endeavours are to prevent the sad
consequences of your disobedience to the calls
of the Gospel. They would pluck you,
by all the means in their power, as brands
from the burning, and are doing exactly what
you would do by them, or by any fellow-crea-
ture the most indifferent, were you to perceive
them literally in such danger. Knowing that
they must shortly leave you, and go the way
of all the earth, they would fain have the
parting pangs mitigated by the animating
prospect of their beloved children following
them, " who through faith and patience are
about to inherit the promises." They have
had their share of earthly sorrows, nevertheless they have found that " wisdom's ways
are ways of pleasantness, and that all her
paths are peace." These paths they wish,
above all things, to see you tread : if you
deviate from them, they know that it is at
your peril; that you are persisting in what

will eventually prove itself to be an evil and
a destructive course. Perhaps even the reluc-
tance which you evince to submit to their
government, they deplore more on your account than on their own, as it manifests a
spirit of rebellion against a higher power.
David viewed things in this light, when under
a deep sense of his sin towards a fellow-crea-
ture he exclaimed, " Against thee—thee *only*
have I sinned, and done this evil." They
cannot bear you to live at enmity with Him,
whose wrath is so dreadful; who to His enemies is " a consuming fire; to His own people a Father of mercies—a God of consolation.

If your parents have had a religious education themselves, suffer not this circumstance
(in itself so favourable) to prejudice your
judgment, nor thus attempt to pervert a family
blessing into a curse, as though they must
necessarily have taken up their opinions as a
matter of course, because they were taught
them in their childhood. David says, as a
confirmation of his faith, " Our fathers trusted in thee;" and *his* religion was certainly
not the effect of habit and prejudice, for like

many now a-days, who can also boast of
pious ancestry, he had for himself " sought
out" the ways of God, and he *knew* by reflection and experience that they were "just and
true."

Nor are principles to be lightly relinquished, because those who urge them may not be
eminently skilled in their defence; they may
be weak champions in combating the sophis-
try of infidelity, who yet prove that they are
strong Christians by their consistent profession : like one who said, " I cannot argue for
Christ, but I can die for him." They may be
able to give a *good* reason of the hope that is
in them, although it may not be such a one
as shall satisfy a captious doubter. It is possible even that their *creed* is correct: and one
that has been adopted by such a host of wor-
thies for so many ages, must not be hastily
or contemptuously discarded.

The mention of a throne of grace to irre-
ligious persons, is, if not literally unintelligible, at least adopting a phraseology at which
they scoff: yet thither the names of graceless
children are often carried with " O that Ish-
mael might live before thee!" And thither

too in answer to their prayers, those very
children are often found to repair and sue in
their own persons for the mercy which once
they rejected.   " Thy people shall be willing
in the day of thy power." May that propitious
day be at hand, when those young readers
who are yet afar off shall be brought nigh,
whether they be among the lukewarm and
careless, or rank with the dissipated and pro-
fane; or whether they class with those who,
from a love of dissipation and worldly pleasure, endeavour to persuade themselves that
they disbelieve Christianity: this is a common process, for

> " Ills in the life breed errors in the brain,
> And these, reciprocally, those again."

But whatever be the kind or degree of
their aversion to religion, whenever they shall
return and seek the God of their fathers, they
will find him compassionate and full of mercy.
Even now, while they are afar off, he is ready
to meet them with a full pardon and a free
welcome.   " Good and upright is the Lord,
therefore will He teach *sinners* in the way."

But let us reverse the picture.   There are

many who, notwithstanding every obstacle,
every hindrance from within and from without, resolutely maintain their religious course,
even while their parents remain enemies to
God. (They would probably feel indignant
at being so designated; but " he that is not
for Him is against Him." The worldly mind
is enmity to God, whatever specious appearance it may assume.) But should you, my
young friend, be the child of such parents,
suffer not spiritual pride to alloy the purity of
that religion which you are solicitous to recommend, the chief character of which is to
be meek and lowly: for " who made you to
differ?" " or what have you that you have
not received?" The cause you would support may sustain the greatest injury, by your
assuming that superiority over your parents
which genuine religion will not sanction. If
you are a real disciple of Jesus, you will aim
to be like Him; nor will you adopt that carriage towards your fellow-creatures, much
less towards those whom His providence has
set over you, which he never displayed even
when surrounded by persecutors, and although
He was Lord of all.

H

You are, indeed, placed in delicate circumstances, which require that " the wisdom of the serpent should be blended with the harmlessness of the dove :" for if the constancy you evince in maintaining your liberty of conscience is liable to misconstruction, probably much more liable would be any attempts on your part to enlighten the minds of your parents; such endeavours should be made with the utmost circumspection, delicacy, and address; and perhaps after all, the most effectual method that can be adopted in such a case, is the cultivation of those christian graces which adorn the doctrine you profess : these will more effectually recommend it than all *you* can urge in its behalf. Let your religion reflect such a radiant lustre all around, that not only your parents, but all within your sphere, " may see your good works, and so learn to glorify your Father which is in heaven."

CHAP. XI.

THE DEATH OF PARENTS.

———

" And when Jacob had made an end of commanding his sons, he gathered up his feet into the bed, and yielded up the ghost, and was gathered unto his people.

GENESIS, xlix. 33.

" And Joseph fell upon his Father's face, and wept upon him, and kissed him."

GENESIS, l. 1.

———

EVERY fresh stage in the life of man is important, especially as he is connected with others by natural ties; and with parents, each increases in interest as their families advance towards maturity. When they have disposed of them in life, when they have dandled their children's children on their knees, then another interesting event—the most interesting of all awaits them. Having set their house in or-

H 2

der, they must prepare to depart, and take up
their abode in *that house* which is appointed
for all living, where the busy scenes of life
are over, and where, whatever once employed
their most strenuous exertions in this busy
world, concerns them no longer. As when
we entered it we brought nothing with us, so
it is certain when we quit it we can carry
nothing away; and this consideration should
have due weight with those who possess property to leave behind them, that their succes-
sors may have no just occasion for complaint,
nor be involved in domestic disputes by an
unfair distribution of it. That the death of
parents should be the signal for bitter ani-
mosities and contentions among surviving
children, is truly unnatural and indecent.
Carry not your resentment, my dear reader,
against any individual of your family to the
borders of the grave—the confines of an eternal world, forgetting that beyond it is the bar
of final equity This would be to make the
last act of your life an act of sin, and perhaps
to entail miseries on your family, when re-
dressing them will be for ever out of your
power.   Neither by weak superstition, nor

criminal procrastination, suffer your property
to pass into hands for which you never designed it. *Set thine house in order*—leave it
not in confusion if you would be remembered
with respect by your survivors. It is " the
memory of the *just* only that is blessed."

To have the loins girded and the lamp
burning ready to depart, is the grand aim of
every true Christian ;—happy those, who when
their Lord cometh He shall find so prepared.
To behold a venerable saint, who has " accomplished as an hireling his day" on the confines
of both worlds, is the most interesting and
instructive scene that our eyes can behold.
Let imagination pourtray a weeping family
surrounding the bed of a departing christian
mother :—by every tender office that affection
can devise, they endeavour to mitigate the
pangs of expiring nature,—she still views
them with maternal feelings, elevated by the
glowing sentiments of a happy spirit on the
confines of immortality—she gazes till their
still-loved forms become indistinct—they re-
cede from her view—celestial objects steal on
her sight—she closes her eyes on mortal
things—she wings her way to regions un-

known, and her weeping family quit the silent chamber.

Are there any among the mourning groupe who have never suffered their imaginations to realize such an event?—They have been aware, indeed, that "it is appointed for all men once to die," and have known that their parents, in common with all the human race, must one day take their departure; so that " the place that once knew them, shall know them no more for ever:" but such vague ideas afford no accurate conception of the reality. Now they behold that countenance, which once exhibited expressions of tender affection, of anxious solicitude, perhaps sometimes of disapprobation or of grief, unmeaning and inanimate, whether it be gazed upon by children once dutiful or undutiful—by friends or by foes.

> " This languishing head is at rest,
>   Its thinking and aching are o'er ;
> This quiet immoveable breast
>   Is heaved by affliction no more.
> This heart is no longer the seat
>   Of trouble, and torturing pain ;
> It ceases to flutter and beat ;
>   It never shall flutter again."

A few more gloomy days, and the sad remains
will be deposited in their " long home," and
the survivors will be left to their reflections.
Many there are who in such circumstances will
experience a sweet mitigation of their sorrows,
in the recollection of their past conduct ; and
some there may be, to whom the retrospect can
afford little satisfaction. Is there a reader who
has been remiss in attention to a drooping
parent, whose heartless services must have
been well understood, and keenly felt by her
who was so well skilled in the offices of kindness? Every apartment of the house, almost
every common circumstance of the day, may
bring to the recollection scenes which would
gladly be recalled, or forgotten.   " It was in
this room," may such a one say, " that I so
grieved her spirit by my pert or rebellious
carriage.—In that chair she sat, when I refused
to comply with such her request—I do not
now think it was unreasonable.   It was there
that I witnessed her feeble air and languid
look, when, instead of offering my services, I
turned away in quest of my own pleasures.
This, and this, and this, are tokens of love I
received from her on various occasions—Oh I

shall value them more than ever now! It is
just so long since she complied with my
wishes, evidently for peace, sake. This is the
room in which she watched over my bed
during my tedious sickness: methinks I see
her anxious looks, her unremitting care, as
though she was guarding the choicest treasure.
Unhappy me! My grief admits of no cure—I
will follow my injured mother in sorrow to
the grave.—But stay—I will go to my afflicted father, and pour the balm of filial consolation into his bereaved bosom. Departed
saint!—If you *can* look down on mortals once
dear to you, behold your repenting child, rendering that tribute of duty to your torn and
lonely partner which was once your due.—
Yes, if aught in this lower world can assuage
his bleeding wounds and mitigate his woes,
the task shall be mine to administer that consolation.—If aught can mitigate or assuage
my own, it must be the tender offices of filial
love, which I will ever render him till he joins
your happy spirit in the mansions above."

We would hope there are few comparatively to whom the former part of this soli-
loquy would be at all applicable; but there

are none, having a surviving parent duly
sensible of his loss who may not adopt the
latter. Their utmost assiduities, although
unable to heal such a wound, may do
much towards mitigating the smart. To whom
can parents look for comfort when thus
bereaved, with such reasonable expectation
as to their own offspring? On whom have they
such imperious claims? If children did but
consult their own interests, they would by
their attentive and affectionate conduct often
prevent the necessity for second marriages,
and parents would not be forced to solicit happiness from strangers, because it cannot be
found in the bosom of their own families!

CHAP. XII.

" What wilt thou give me, seeing I go childless."

GENESIS, xv. 2.

ALTHOUGH the preceding pages have been
exclusively addressed to *parents and children,*
a few words to those who stand in neither of
those relations, it is hoped will not be deemed
so unpardonable a digression, as to be altogether unacceptable.

There are those who have had years of
married life embittered, because it has pleased
Providence to withhold from them a family,
and who, while they hear others complain of
the various trials to which they are thereby exposed, are ready to think that such troubles are
not to be compared with their own, "so foolish
are we, and ignorant!" So apt to forget that

" the heart knoweth its own bitterness." The hackneyed methods of consolation have probably hitherto been tried in vain; in vain they hear, that the ill-inclined and vicious, the amiable and deserving, severally excite in the bosoms of parents the deepest sorrow, although on very opposite accounts: the misconduct of the former, the misfortunes of the latter, each rending their hearts and banishing their repose. They hear, that in all their afflictions we are afflicted, and that our anxieties multiply with our children. Let childless persons who repine at their lot, read the heart-rending lamentation of David over a rebellious Absalom, or hear him in bitter anguish supplicating for the life of a dying infant! Let them attend to the pathetic story of Rispah, the daughter of Aiah, who watched night and day the corpses of her slain family, and they will no longer attempt to say that " there is no sorrow like unto their sorrow;" especially if they recollect that to these, or woes equally bitter, every parent is liable. But this is not a view of the subject calculated to afford solid consolation: that can be derived only from an humble submission to

the all-wise disposer of events, who both gives
and withholds, in subservience to the best
interests of his people. The time is at hand
when those who have wives, and husbands,
and children, shall be as though they had
them not; and then, although you may not
literally be entitled to say, " here am I, and
the children thou hast given me." You may,
nevertheless, bring up a long train to join in
the triumph of that day, who may own you
as their spiritual parents, as the honoured instruments of their new birth unto God. In
such an animating prospect Paul gloried, although he had probably neither sons nor
daughters, according to the flesh; and well
he might, and well may every zealous pro-
moter of the Gospel of Christ rejoice, for
" whoever converts a sinner from the error
of his ways, shall shine as the stars in the fir-
mament for ever and ever."

Remember then, my dear reader, that although Providence has withheld from you
the pleasures and the cares of a family, as a
Christian you may have other pleasures, and
should have other cares; your responsibility,
although altered in its character, is not di

minished. Should you see the work of the
Lord prosper in your hands, happy are you.
It is evidently His pleasure, that the talents
with which you are intrusted should be directed into a foreign channel. It will be well
if you are enabled to co-operate with his wise
designs. " He will give you a name better
than that of sons and of daughters."

The same all-wise disposer has seen fit to
" take away from others the desire of their
eyes with a stroke;" to level all their pleasing anticipations with the dust! ere the tender bud had unfolded—or just as it had begun
to disclose its varied tints—or when a full-
blown flower, the pride of the parterre, and
distinguished among the neighbouring plants
for fragrance and beauty! To hearts thus
lacerated and still bleeding, what healing
balm can be applied? what cordial administered, sufficient to revive the drooping
spirits? Will it suffice to tell the disconsolate
mourners (as some officiously do) that all
their grief is unavailing, as it cannot bring
back the object of it? This were to mock their
woes, and to affront their understandings. Nor
is it less vain to form a thousand chimerical

suppositions of what calamities *might* have
befallen the deceased, had their lives been
prolonged, or what unfavourable characters
they *might* have proved, since it is clear that
none of these things were ever designed, any
more than that they might have proved comforts to their parents and ornaments to society;
—suppositions which would be quite as rational, and much more charitable. But to
those who have no better consolations to
offer, it may justly be said, " miserable com-
forters are ye all." Such antidotes'for grief
are often tried, but never succeed. A bleeding heart is not to be *so* healed; and he who
alone can do it effectually, might say to those
who attempt it, " Ye have healed the hurt of
the daughter of my people slightly." It is he
alone who can administer true consolation to
the afflicted, whether he denies children, or
takes them away, or chastises us in or
through them. His divine supports under
painful dispensations " calm the surges of
the mind," and afford consolation of the most
effectual kind. The assurance " that all
things shall work together for good," and
that " these light afflictions, which are but

for a moment, work out a far more exceeding and eternal weight of glory," ever retain their value, however common and familiar they may be to the ear They are calculated to produce a cheerful acquiescence in the divine will; not, indeed, if such passages are read carelessly and without reflection: it is only when we pause, and endeavour to receive their full meaning, that their efficacy is felt.

But although with what children *might* have been, a bereaved parent has nothing to do, yet abundant consolation may be derived in many cases from the contemplation of what they now *are*. Happy spirits!—removed from the parental embrace to repose on the bosom of Jesus, where they can never be assailed by sickness or sorrow, and where they cannot die any more.

The writer will here take the liberty to recommend a little volume, entitled, " The Mourner," by Dr. Grosvenor, admirably adapted to such occasions. May the bereaved and broken-hearted, and disappointed, experience the truth of that promise which says, " Though He hath torn, He will also heal!"

CHAP. XIII.

THE ORPHAN.

------

*" When my father and my mother forsake me, then
the Lord will take me up.*   PSALM, xxvii. 10.

YOUNG persons, living in ease and affluence
in their father's house, do not always calcu-
late for the future; but are disposed to think
that " to-morrow shall be as this day, and
much more abundant." It has, perhaps,
never occurred to some, by what a precarious
tenure they hold their present enjoyments;
that they may be essentially curtailed, if not
totally annihilated by the death of their parents; that on the fleeting breath in their
nostrils, depend those appearances on which
they so greatly value themselves; that by this
alone their gay families may be preserved from
a state of poverty or dependance. But even

where this is not the case, such a mournful
event generally throws the younger branches
of a family in a greater or a less degree on the
care and benevolence of others. A more habitual sense of our precarious enjoyment of
earthly friends would produce very salutary
effects on the conduct and character of young
persons, who, satisfied with present compe-
tence and security, have not learned to calcu-
late on a sudden reverse of circumstances,
when they may be obliged for advice and protection, perhaps even support, to those whom
they now view with indifference, if not dis-
dain; or when they may meet with disinterested and needful friendship, from quarters
where their present conduct cannot at all entitle them to expect it. Common policy (not
to mention higher principles) would suggest
these sentiments, as we cannot tell whose
services we may need. It is " the prudent
who foresee the evil, while the simple pass
on and are punished."

The vicissitudes of human life are such,
that it is wise to be prepared for all changes;
and the young, while secure and happy beneath the parental roof, should be careful by

an amiable and conciliating conduct to engage the good will and esteem of all around :
that is a prudent resolution, which the young
reader has perhaps been taught to adopt.

> " Though I'm now in younger days,
> Nor can tell what shall befall me,
> I'll prepare for every place
> Where my growing age shall call me."

The death of parents is certainly the severest calamity with which either infancy, or
childhood, or youth, can be visited : having
no claim on new guardians or protectors
equal to that of natural affection, the orphan
who has found such protectors should not be
wanting in a grateful sense and expression of
the obligation ; especially should a sentiment
of fervent gratitude be kindled towards that
Being, who, having the hearts of all at His
disposal, raises up friends for the destitute,
and " setteth the solitary in families " But
should He in His wisdom have seen fit to
withhold for the present all human aid, and
seemed to have cast them on the mercy of a
cold world, " His tender mercies are over *all*
His works," and the *orphan* is the object of

His peculiar regard. He is so eminently the
father of the fatherless, that there have been
none, however circumstanced, who might
not eventually have reared their Ebenezer,
saying, " Hitherto the Lord hath helped
me." Should you, at present, appear to be
cast on the wide world with none but God
for your friend, what need you more? It
was not a destitute orphan, but the king of
Israel who exclaimed, " Whom have *I* in
heaven but thee? and there is none on earth
that I desire beside thee." He knew he de-
pended upon God as much for protection
and support as one of the meanest of his subjects. And you, with equal confidence, may
lay claim to the same fatherly care.

But whatever be our situation, however
great our faith, and sincere our dependance,
we must still expect our share of earthly sorrows; they will assuredly assail us, however
we may be supported under them, or eventually delivered from them :—especially the
true Christian must expect them, for whom
the Lord loveth, He chasteneth. The orphan
has peculiar promises, but they are not such
as can assure him of health, or riches, or

favour with the world.   But while he hum-
bly depends upon the assurance, his bread
will be given, and his water *will* be sure. " I
have not seen the righteous forsaken." "Seek
not" then, my young friend, " great things
for yourself" in this world, but set your affections on higher objects—on things above ;
and then you will know both how to want
and how to abound, and " in whatever state
you are therewith to be content."

If there is reason to hope that your departed parents had thus been " made wise to
salvation," let it quicken you to " be follow-
ers of them, who through faith and patience
inherit the promises." A few more revolving
seasons, and you also must quit this busy
scene, with all its anxieties and sorrows.
Your bones may be deposited beside them, but
they will there bid you no welcome—the knees
on which you were once dandled, the arms
which once encircled you, are motionless in
death—the eyes which gazed on you with
delight, are for ever closed—the hand which
administered to your wants, has " forgot its
cunning." It is in the mansions above that
you will unite again, with all your powers

and faculties infinitely improved; your painful wanderings through this troublesome world
will then be forgotten, or only remembered
with gratitude to your great deliverer. There
will be no more trying vicissitudes or painful
separations, but faithful parents and dutiful
children will unite in ceaseless praises to the
universal Parent. Let the afflicted in all circumstances " comfort one another with these
words."

CONCLUSION.

———

" Our babes shall richest comforts bring;
If tutor'd right, they'll prove a spring
   Whence pleasures ever rise:
We'll form their minds with studious care
To all that's manly, good, and fair,
   And train them for the skies.

While they our wisest hours engage,
They'll joy our youth, support our age,
   And crown our hoary hairs:
They'll grow in virtue every day,
And thus our fondest loves repay,
   And recompense our cares."

COTTON.

———

IT has been attempted in the preceding pages to suggest some hints for the promotion of domestic happiness; those which remain shall be occupied in pointing out that upon which alone any reasonable hope of success can be founded—namely, *early discipline.*

Parents and children naturally expect to derive mutual comfort from those intimate relations; but wishes and expectations are fruitless without corresponding exertions, and even exertions may prove ineffectual if delayed beyond their proper season. Were parents sufficiently convinced of this, what happy effects would result to society in general, as well as to their own immediate circle! It is in the *nursery* that their operations must first commence, if they would look forward to distant years, with any reasonable hope of deriving comfort from the society of their grown-up children.

It may be objected that many bright examples might be produced, to prove that excellence of character does not always depend on early education; and on the contrary, that some undutiful, and even profligate children have been in these respects highly favoured: but such instances are only exceptions; without which there is no general rule; and such exceptions (those especially of the latter class) are very rare. Let the assertion then sink deep into the heart of every parent. *The foundation stone of public*

and private felicity should be laid in the nur-
sery, not by the mercenary services of ignorant domestics, but by the skilful hand of the
intelligent christian *mother.* In that insigni-
ficant chamber, bestrewed with fragments of
toys and glittering baubles, the scene of
frolic and gambol, resounding with the tones
of infantile mirth and woe,—the future happiness or misery of the fire-side below is (if
we may be allowed the expression) manufac-
tured, which may spread from thence far
and wide. It is here that filial respect, filial
affection, with all their accompanying virtues,
although small at first as a grain of mustard-
seed, begin to spring: the twigs shoot forth,
the blossoms appear, delicious fruits ripen
on the boughs, and, harbouring every tuneful
songster, from thence shall issue many a
melodious strain. It is here that humility
and self-denial first break the stubborn soil,
and expand their tender foliage like the snow-
drop and violet, those welcome flowers of
spring. Here with needful culture, prudence,
and discretion, and benevolence display the
promising bud, while the assiduous and skilful hand will clear from the ground every

noxious weed which would retard or destroy their growth. And here especially, as the grand source of all, should be first sown the good seed of the word, which if dressed and watered by the prayers and tears of a pious parent, may even here spring up and bear its early fruit. On this interesting spot are often planted the thorns which protrude from a parent's dying pillow, or the sweet flowerets which bestrew it.

What a comprehensive term is domestic happiness! It includes the important present—it involves the future to an indefinite extent: to generations yet unborn its benign influence extends, beyond the reach of calculation.

> " If solid happiness we prize,
> Within our breast this jewel lies;
>   And they are fools who roam:
> The world has nothing to bestow;
> From our own selves our joys must flow,
>   And that dear hut our *home*."

If it would not warrant the philanthropist to devote the best of *his* time, *his* talents, *his* exertions to the grand object within the limits of his own walls, it might justify *her*

1

in so doing whose peculiar province it is.
While other things are not neglected, let
home duties be the primary concern with her.
Could the writer of these humble pages have
as many years added to her life as she has
already counted, this important subject,
whenever she ventured to address her sex,
would still constitute the essence of her
counsel.

Let not the above sentiments, however,
be supposed to intimate that the prior duties
of the wife and mother are to seclude her
entirely from all intercourse with the world,
or exclude those of a more diffusive benevolence. On the latter subject there are two
opposite errors, against which the mistresses
of families should carefully guard. While
some from a love of going abroad, of public
assemblies, of bustle, of any thing but stay-
ing at home (and it is hoped from some mix-
ture of better motives), are ever to be seen on
all those occasions, which the present state of
the religious world renders so frequent;
others from the pressure of private cares and
family duties, would excuse themselves not
only from personal activity, but from taking
any interest in the good works that are going

on around them. But let such remember,
that he who said to David, concerning his
zeal for the Lord's house, " Thou didst well
in that it was in thine heart," can, and does
distinguish between indifference to His service, and inability to engage in it. In the
primitive times of Christianity, those women
only were accounted worthy of regard who,
besides " guiding the house and bringing up
children," had also " lodged strangers and
washed the saints' feet," and who " were
well reported of for good works." There are,
perhaps, some good housewives now-a-days,
who would have been inclined to take Martha s part, and to condemn Mary for her
neglect of household affairs; but Martha was
not reproved for providing a hospitable meal
for her Lord, but for being engrossed about
the non-essentials of it. And it is only those
who, like her, are cumbered with their
private concerns,—or, in other words, cumbered with worldliness of mind, who cannot
find time even to wish and pray for the success of the benevolent exertions of others.

An instance just now occurs to our recollection (doubtless by no means a singular one)
of a pious woman, who besides the charge of a

large young family, was an active assistant
to her husband in a flourishing trade. If any
circumstances could warrant inattention to
out-door duties, they are such as these; but
she did not avail herself of these excuses.
While she was an affectionate mother, and
governed her children and her servants with
discretion; while she was diligent in business,
and attentive to her customers, she always
manifested a lively interest in the labours of
love that were carried on in the Christian
society to which she belonged. She could
not herself do much, but what she *could,* she
did. She encouraged others who were more
at leisure than herself. She was willing to
contribute of her substance to the good cause.
She found time occasionally to visit her poor
and sick neighbours, proving the truth of the
vulgar adage, that, " where there is a will
there is a way." Nor will this be thought
wonderful when it is added, that the time
which many persons in her condition spend
in frivolous pursuits, was saved by her for
better purposes. She dressed herself and her
children in a manner becoming her station, and
therefore she had both the time and the money
which others so vainly squander to spare for

the cause of God and her neighbour. The reader will excuse this digression.

To return to the subject :—whether we take a general view of human nature as it appears abroad in the world, or a more intimate survey of it from the knowledge of ourselves, and of those immediately within our sphere, it might be expected to operate as a forcible lesson on all to whom Providence has intrusted the culture of the rising generation. Can parents look around them, and take no alarm at the follies and vices which they behold on every side? Do they imagine the moral habits in which their children are nurtured, must of course secure them from the contagion? Can they be supine and indifferent amid the evils they are every hour compelled to witness, and by which their own happiness is so frequently disturbed? Whence originally proceed those crosses and vexations, those goads in our sides which occasion such frequent complaints of this troublesome world? Not from the *immediate* hand of Providence, which does not shower down even upon guilty creatures an uninterrupted storm; but would permit them to enjoy many a serene, if not a cloudless day. No, they are woes

which we inflict upon each other. It is true
we are thus made instruments in His hand,
by which He frequently chastises us; yet He
authorises—nay, He *commands* us to use all
our endeavours by education, to convert these
swords into ploughshares, these spears into
pruning-hooks; to render what is hostile and
dangerous, useful and beneficial; and this will
assuredly be required at our hands.

It were vain to attempt to enforce such
sentiments on self-approving Pharisees, by
the contemplation of their own depraved propensities: their ostentatious boasts, that "they
are not as other men," drive us to make our
appeal to the experienced Christian. Those
who feel and bewail the disorder within their
own bosoms, can make a salutary application
of the principle in the case of their offspring.
They see their work before them at greater certainty, and they apply themselves to it with unremitting energy and zeal. They apply *themselves* to it, so far as their talents and opportunities permit them: the want of these, in many
instances, demands a substitute for parental
exertions. Yet surely the christian mother
will be solicitous, at least, to superintend the
moral culture of her charge during the first

years of life   The general admonition, " to look well to our flocks and our herds," she applies to the care of those tender lambs which are exposed during infancy to innumerable perils, from which few hands but those of a mother can defend them. She is solicitous, at least, to lay the foundation of a structure which shall be proof against the boisterous winds, the beating rain, and the swelling flood : having so done, there is less danger in committing the *external* decorations of the building to other hands.   But those who neglect to do this, or attempt it too late, or perform it unskilfully, or trust too implicitly to the services of others, must not complain of their hard lot, as though some strange thing had befallen them, when they reap the inevitable consequences.   It would be much more strange were not their natural effects to follow such causes.

At the conduct of the world in these re-spects we cannot wonder ; but what shall we say to those who, making higher pretensions than a common profession of christianity ; those who afford us some reason to hope that they have indeed embraced the Gospel of Christ, and know something of its power, as

well as of its doctrines; yet so grievously
fall short of the spirit of it in the management of their offspring? The head of a family assembles his household together for
worship—he opens the sacred volume, and
reads the history of Eli, and of Eli's family: he
closes the book, and like a man beholding his
natural face in a glass, and afterwards forgetting what manner of person he is, goes his
way without making any salutary application
of it: although, alas! it is more than the
united efforts of the mother and the servants
have been able to effect, to restrain his boisterous children, or to maintain a decent
silence during the short interval of religious
worship!

Be it the ambition then of every true Christian to make his house a seminary, in which
citizens are educated for the present world; a
temple, in which they are early dedicated to,
and prepared for the world to come.

THE END.

T. Miller, Printer, 5, Noble Street, Cheapside.

Printed in the United States
By Bookmasters